John Lyons is an acclaimed jo[...]
Editor at the Australian Broadca[...]
over three decades of experience in international journalism,
Lyons has reported from some of the world's most turbulent
regions, including the Middle East and Ukraine. His insightful
reporting has earned him numerous awards, including four
prestigious Walkley Awards for Excellence in Journalism, and
he has twice been named Australian Journalist of the Year.

Lyons is known for his deep analysis and compelling
storytelling, bringing the human aspects of global conflicts to the
forefront. He is the author of *Balcony Over Jerusalem*, an account of
his time in the Middle East covering the Israel–Palestine conflict.

This latest work, based on his three trips to cover the Ukraine
War, offers a poignant look into the lives of everyday civilians
caught in the crossfire, showcasing their resilience and spirit.

A Bunker in Kyiv

JOHN LYONS WITH SYLVIE LE CLEZIO

ABC
BOOKS

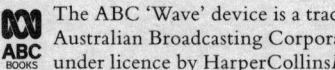 The ABC 'Wave' device is a trademark of the
Australian Broadcasting Corporation and is used
under licence by HarperCollins*Publishers* Australia.

HarperCollins*Publishers*
Australia • Brazil • Canada • France • Germany • Holland • India
Italy • Japan • Mexico • New Zealand • Poland • Spain • Sweden
Switzerland • United Kingdom • United States of America

HarperCollins acknowledges the Traditional Custodians
of the lands upon which we live and work, and pays respect
to Elders past and present.

First published on Gadigal Country in Australia in 2025
by HarperCollins*Publishers* Australia Pty Limited
ABN 36 009 913 517
harpercollins.com.au

HarperCollins*Publishers*
Macken House, 39/40 Mayor Street Upper
Dublin 1, D01 C9W8, Ireland

A catalogue record for this book is available from the National Library of Australia

ISBN 978 1 4607 6782 5 (paperback)
ISBN 978 1 4607 1733 2 (ebook)

Cover design by Louisa Maggio, HarperCollins Design Studio
Cover and internal photographs by Sylvie Le Clezio unless noted otherwise
Typeset in Baskerville MT Pro by Kirby Jones

Printed and bound by CPI Group (UK) Ltd, Croydon, CR0 4YY

To the people of Ukraine who stood up when their country needed them. They have shown extraordinary resilience, courage and grace under pressure.

CONTENTS

Author's note   ix

Introduction   1

1   Day zero   21

2   A citizen army   51

3   Life in wartime   88

4   Medical marvels   133

5   Children of the war   155

6   Cyber fighters   180

7   The drone busters   203

8   The leader: Zelensky   220

9   The enemy: Putin   242

10   The deal maker: Trump   272

Acknowledgements   303

Endnotes   307

AUTHOR'S NOTE

I AM WRITING THESE WORDS THREE YEARS TO THE DAY since Russia launched its full-scale invasion of Ukraine, starting the first land war in Europe since World War II. Ukraine's President Volodymyr Zelensky – who has held his country together in the face of this assault by the fourth-largest army in the world – has just offered to resign his presidency if that would mean that Ukraine could be admitted to NATO.

Today is also four weeks since Donald Trump returned to the White House and began overturning long-held assumptions of how the US acts on a global scale. Judging by early indications, the second Trump presidency will shape up to be the most radical in US history.

Trump has so far renamed the Gulf of Mexico the 'Gulf of America', raised the idea of Canada becoming America's 51st state, threatened to take Greenland by force, and set off a political earthquake in the Middle East by suggesting the US could 'own' Gaza and turn it into a real-estate development. On Gaza – already one of the most sensitive pieces of land in the world – Trump talked about 'cleaning' it out, urging neighbouring countries to take in the 2.3 million displaced Palestinians, who have just endured 15 months of Israeli bombing.

He then unleashed a storm in Ukraine, accusing President Zelensky of being a dictator and said that Ukraine had started the war – a demonstrable untruth. These comments shocked people around the world, particularly European leaders, who may feel it is now up to them to try to save Ukraine from Russia's invasion. When those European leaders defended Zelensky, Trump turned his gaze to them, accusing French President Emmanuel Macron and British Prime Minister Sir Keir Starmer of not doing enough to help Ukraine.

Ukraine has put up a remarkable resistance to the might of the Russian army. In his statements, Trump made clear the US is considering withdrawing support for Ukraine. If European countries did the same, Ukraine would fall within weeks or months – exactly what Putin had hoped when he invaded on 24 February 2022. Russia's violence and war crimes – enabled by the Kremlin sending tens of thousands of young Russians to the meat grinder of the front line – would be rewarded with the subsummation of Ukraine into Putin's planned restoration of a Russian empire.

Trump's actions now put in doubt Ukraine's long-term survival. But what has never been in doubt is the determination, resilience and dignity of the Ukrainian people. Without their remarkable efforts, Vladimir Putin would have already taken Kyiv, and the whole country with it.

This book looks at how a nation of 44 million people swung into action to save their country. It documents the extraordinary efforts of those ordinary Ukrainians, showcasing a people rising to levels that they never realised they were capable of when confronted with tragedy and an existential threat to their existence.

The future of Ukraine will not be decided quickly. Whatever Donald Trump and the European leaders decide, Ukrainians will fight to the end to fend off this threat to their sovereignty. The passion for independence burns within the souls of Ukrainians.

John Lyons
24 February 2025

INTRODUCTION

IT'S THE MIDDLE OF THE NIGHT AND I'M WRITING THIS from a bunker in Ukraine. Russians have just fired a new barrage of missiles towards us and no-one is sure where they're going to land. The air-raid sirens in Lviv went off a few minutes ago, echoing around the eerie darkness of this magnificent historic city. I've just left the capital, Kyiv, where I've been based for the last month, and thought that here in western Ukraine I'd be spared the almost nightly missile attacks, finally getting an uninterrupted night's sleep without having to doze on a beanbag (if I'm quick enough to get one) in a Kyiv bunker.

How wrong I was. In Ukraine these days, there's nowhere to hide. Vladimir Putin's war machine is relentless. The hard men of the Kremlin spare no-one.

Those of us staying in the hotel have crowded into this bunker behind reception on the ground floor. We're not sure if the attack is from cruise missiles or Shahid drones, which can be loaded with up to forty kilograms of explosives. We're all studying our phones, scanning the various apps that update in real time about what has been fired and the origins of the attacks. Often the missiles are fired from Russian jets flying over Belarus or ships in the Caspian or Black seas.

If the Russians fire a cruise missile from the Caspian Sea, you have up to forty minutes to get into a bunker. Cruise missiles and drones are pretty standard fare in this war; if people see them on their phones, no-one panics. What you never want to see on your screen is the word 'Kinzhal'. Kinzhals are to missiles what taipans are to snakes, the deadliest of all. They are hypersonic missiles, and their lethality comes from the fact that they travel at 12,350 kilometres per hour. If the Russians fire one of these, you have only five minutes to take cover. Your chances of surviving a Kinzhal is small.

The Americans have an extraordinary satellite system based in neighbouring Poland that is assisting Ukraine to monitor its skies. The moment it detects a Russian MIG jet, which has the capability to launch a Kinzhal, preparing to take off, the American military command in Warsaw alerts Ukrainian air defence, who set off nationwide alarms that send everyone scrambling to bunkers or underground train stations. But just because MIGs can carry a Kinzhal doesn't mean they actually are. The Americans and Ukrainians know it might be a false alarm, but it's better to err on the side of caution than risk not having enough time to get into a bunker should a Kinzhal actually be launched. It's better for children to be taken from their beds one hundred times on false alarms than risk the one time when a Kinzhal may actually be headed their way. This war is as much about playing with the mind of the enemy as it is firing hardware.

For the Russians, merely having a MIG taxi along the runway and take off in Belarus, even if it returns in five minutes, brings dividends to Moscow. It forces parents in Ukraine to take their children into a bunker in the middle of the night. It forces carers in nursing homes to rush the bedridden or wheelchair-bound elderly into shelters. It forces staff in hospitals to move sick patients, complete with oxygen tanks and any other equipment, into safer locations. Playing with the mind of the enemy is part of Russia's long game, wearing down Ukrainians over time so that one day, hopefully, they break. And they can do this without firing a missile by just getting a MIG to do a loop or two over an airport in Belarus. For Vladmir Putin, war can be entertaining.

Tonight we're not sure exactly what's being launched at us. The disturbing reality for those of us huddling in this bunker is that Putin, the man authorising the firing of these missiles and drones, has 5977 nuclear warheads at his disposal, more than any other world leader. Many say Putin would never use nuclear weapons. Many also said he would never invade Ukraine. It may well be true – hopefully it *is* true – that he will never use his nuclear arsenal, but that is Putin's decision. How confident can we be in Putin's judgment and stability? As disturbing as it is, we now have a new reality: the world's future is entirely in Putin's hands should he decide to 'go nuclear'.

In this little bunker behind the reception desk of a hotel in central Lviv, we're making a brief and unglamorous cameo in one of history's great dramas: the battle between Russian president Vladimir Putin and Ukrainian president Volodymyr Zelensky. One of them will not survive. Each wants the other dead, and if one dies, the other wins. If Putin wins, Ukraine will no longer exist in its current form. It will become, as it was during the Soviet era, a satellite state of Russia. If Zelensky survived such an outcome, he would need to flee Ukraine. If Zelensky wins, Putin's many enemies – including many of Russia's generals and oligarchs with their huge private armies – will almost certainly move against him. Some of those private armies have as many as 50,000 'security officers'.

While most Ukrainians have spent some time in bunkers, many of them are getting on with their lives. On some days during this war, Ukraine has been using the amount of ammunition equivalent to that which all of Europe produces in one day. And yet, on the surface, much of the country appears to be going about its business as usual. By day, Ukraine can seem a sophisticated, well functioning European country. Kyiv defiantly remains an enchanting city – people sitting at cafés on the streets, restaurants busy and high-fashion boutiques doing a good trade. But as the sun disappears, so does normalcy.

Many nights, air-raid sirens ring out, typically at 3 or 4 am when Putin knows they will cause maximum inconvenience. The country goes into nocturnal chaos. If you don't have access to a bunker, it's best to move in to a room that has no windows, often bathrooms. Being in a room with no windows reduces the chance of damage from glass caused by a bomb. Some people I spoke to have taken to pre-emptively sleeping in their bathroom so they don't have to relocate every time they hear a siren, or out of fear they won't wake up in time to run to the safety of the tiled room.

But the next morning, when their ears stop ringing, they turn into a 'volunteer army' of millions of Ukrainians. They use their special talents to carry out activities designed to cause maximum disruption to the Russians, from hacking cyber infrastructure to weaving camouflage tents to adapting agricultural drones for front-line warfare. This is a nation of people who wake each day with the credo, 'What can I do for the war effort today?'

During my time in Ukraine, I discovered tales of inspiration about how the human spirit, challenged by a formidable and violent enemy, can rise up and believe that it will never be beaten. These are stories of human triumph against one of the darkest forces in today's world, of ordinary people doing extraordinary things. This book confronts the images that we have of war, showing that the human spirit can survive almost anything. And now, years into the war, the Ukrainian spirit is stronger than ever.

*

This is a very different book from the one we expected to write. We had not realised the extent to which a civilian population dominated a war effort. While there have been many books about Ukraine and its war with Russia, this book is about something we rarely hear or read about: Ukraine's army of civilians. Ordinary people doing extraordinary things, from old punk rockers, grandmothers, chefs and butchers to university professors and corporate brand managers who are relentlessly working behind the scenes to beat the might of the fourth-largest army in the world.

On paper, Russia should have won this war within days. Military strategists who compared the power of the Russian army to the much smaller army of Ukraine would have concluded that Ukraine would not be able to hold out for very long. Certainly, Vladimir Putin began the war believing what his military command had told him: that Russia could capture the capital within days. The victorious images of Russian troops standing triumphantly in Maidan Square in Kyiv would have boosted the Russian public and solidified Putin as the great Russian leader trying to put the Russian empire back together. The narrative would have been that Russia had 'reclaimed' the largest of the jewels from the old Soviet crown and in the process created more of a buffer against the advancing influence of the North Atlantic Treaty Organization, more commonly known as NATO. This alliance of thirty-two countries from Europe and North America has each other's backs both politically and militarily. The key commitment that all NATO countries sign on to is Article 5 of the NATO agreement: that if one member is attacked, it is the duty of all the others to respond. This is military insurance of the highest order: if a country attacks one of the alliance's smallest members, such as Lithuania, Latvia or Sweden, then they face likely retribution from all NATO countries, including the US. Even though Ukraine is not a NATO member – much to Putin's delight and to Ukrainians' frustrations – being in control of a landmass 1316 kilometres wide that borders four NATO nations would be a huge strategic advantage for Putin.

But what Putin and his military command did not take into account was the resilience and determination of the Ukrainian people. After scrambling for the first forty-eight hours, when Ukrainian fighters with Kalashnikovs faced Russian tanks,

Ukraine as a country regrouped spectacularly. That regrouping allowed the formation of one of the most extraordinary armies in history: Ukraine's informal civilians' army.

I made three trips to Ukraine during the war to document this civilian force. My first trip with the Australian Broadcasting Corporation was for the *Four Corners*[1] television program and the second was a month-long assignment for *ABC News*. During this time I had access to Ukraine's intelligence service, the Security Service of Ukraine, or SBU. I visited Ukraine's cyber co-ordination centre, which reports directly to President Zelensky. I spoke to soldiers who'd spent time in the battle of Bakhmut, the bloodiest of them all. And I travelled around the country to look at how an entire population rallied for the fight of their lives.

But while my first two trips were for my job as the ABC's global affairs editor, the third was during my holidays. I understand that going to a country at war is not everyone's idea of a vacation, but it gave me the chance to genuinely immerse myself in the lives and affairs of Ukrainians from a range of backgrounds. My wife, Sylvie, a documentary filmmaker and photographer, joined me for the third trip. We planned to make a documentary on the behind-the-scenes networks in a modern war. We met in Vienna and booked train tickets to Rzeszów in Poland, then an overnight sleeper cabin to Kyiv. That in itself was a fascinating experience, travelling through the night across a country at war.

It was on this third visit that I got to see a side of the war that I hadn't seen on the other trip. Those first two trips were focused on the dramatic and fast-moving news events. On this trip, I was able to spend time talking to Ukrainians from all walks of life. Over three weeks, instead of travelling to the front line to interview military commanders, we spent time wandering through the capital, in Hostomel, Irpin and Bucha talking to people in cafés, restaurants and offices. During these weeks of meeting people who then referred us to other people, I saw a different side of the city than I originally had as a journalist – one where war wasn't always omnipresent, and when it is, it is woven into daily life instead of being separated from it.

It was on this trip that I really learnt about Ukraine. The first two trips were still important. In addition to columns for the ABC website, appearances on *7.30*, *Insiders*, *The World*, *News Breakfast* and live crosses for the ABC TV News channel and current affairs radio programs *AM* and *PM*, I filed sixty radio news stories, two a day for thirty days. It's important that an Australian audience hears the perspective of Australian reporters, but it's intense and physically exhausting. I remember my ABC colleague Isabella Higgins telling me that when she left Ukraine at the end of a trip, she was so exhausted that she felt like sleeping for a week. I came to realise exactly what she meant. After these trips, the moment I left Ukraine to begin the long journey home, I crashed, doing something I rarely did and sleeping almost the entire flight from Warsaw to Dubai and then Dubai to Sydney.

On that third trip, I needed to do things that 'ordinary Ukrainians' did: go to the supermarket, get cash for my rent, find a barbershop, and work out which buses went where. I learnt more about Ukraine on this trip than the first two combined. Without the demands of work, if I met someone interesting in a café or a shopping centre, I was able to sit with them and talk instead of running off for a live TV cross. On one occasion when I needed a camera card, I asked a young couple at the next table at an outdoor café. They knew of an excellent camera shop in an outer suburb but said it was difficult to get to if you didn't know Kyiv. Before I knew it, they'd ordered an Uber (interestingly, Uber is still operating in war-torn Kyiv) and told me and Sylvie that they would take us there. We spent the next two hours with them, and that conversation taught me more about the level of hatred felt today by Ukrainians towards Russians than the rest of my time in Ukraine.

I knew from years living in New York, Washington and Jerusalem that by spending time with locals you can better report a place. When I was based in New York and Washington as a correspondent for *The Australian*, I took whatever opportunities I could to travel to states such as South Carolina, Arkansas, Texas, Chicago and Kentucky. From these trips I learnt more about what made America tick than living in the bubbles of

Washington and New York. Likewise, as the Middle East correspondent for *The Australian* from 2009 to 2015, I lived for six years in the suburbs of Jerusalem among Israelis, which helped me to understand how they saw their decades-long conflict with Palestinians. Scores of trips to the West Bank helped me to really come to know the mindsets of Palestinians. It was these sorts of insights that helped to inform my book *Balcony Over Jerusalem*,[2] originally published in 2017 and re-released in 2024 to help give context to the latest war in Gaza.

For this book I draw on a lot of the high-level access I got on my first two trips to Ukraine but also heavily on that third trip. I spoke to scores of Ukrainians about what the war meant to them and how their lives had changed. In particular they reflected on how the war led to them drawing from personal reserves they did not even know existed; it took every ounce they had to go up against one of the most formidable armies of our time.

I was able to dig into a side of the Ukraine war that I had not been aware of when reporting as a journalist. The real reason Ukraine has put up such an awesome resistance against Russia's invasion. Why Russia would not win this war easily.

As an active warzone, Ukraine presents many challenges for journalists. Over four decades as a reporter, I've encountered many issues when travelling to conflict zones. One I'll never forget was our pilot having to do a 'corkscrew' landing coming into Baghdad in 2014 to avoid being shot down by enemy fire.

I was flying into Iraq as Middle East correspondent of *The Australian* because the editor had called me in Jerusalem and said, 'Islamic State is within a hundred kilometres of Baghdad. There's a good chance they'll take it. Could you get there as soon as possible?' It was one of those phone calls that only journalists get. Islamic State is one of the most daunting terrorist groups of our time, executing journalists without compunction, so most 'normal' jobs would urge you to get far away as quickly as possible. But not in journalism. And despite spending huge amounts of money, the US-led forces had been unable to secure enough of the land surrounding the airport to allow a normal landing at a low angle, so planes had to make a sharp descent in a corkscrew manner.

As a foreign correspondent I've covered many conflicts: four wars in Gaza, the war in Lebanon between Hezbollah and Israel, a military coup in the Philippines, the war in Sri Lanka between the Tamil Tigers and the army, and uprisings in Iran, Iraq, Syria and Egypt. But I've never seen such a surge of determination by an entire populace to win a war like I did in Ukraine. Ukrainians rallied in a way that was different from anything I've encountered before. Ukraine as a nation rose up to fight for their country when many – including Vladimir Putin – expected it to crumble in days.

This is the story of how 44 million Ukrainians waged a war against Vladimir Putin and his army.

*

I've spent time in many different bunkers in Ukraine. Some are luxurious, with wi-fi, espresso machines and beanbags. Others are simpler, such as the one I sheltered in behind the reception desk in Lviv.

I learnt long ago that because so much of the night can be spent in these bunkers, it's best to come prepared to work. In Kyiv, where I'd been on assignment for the ABC, I'd write my weekly columns from them. I even filmed two pieces to camera in bunkers for our major evening TV news.

But tonight, as I open my laptop and begin writing, I see an image that will stay with me. A family arrives. The father carries the younger boy, who I'm later told is aged two. The mother is in a hotel dressing gown, presumably because she's had to rush down here in her pyjamas. They have an older boy who's seven and absorbed in a game on an iPad.

The family is Ukrainian, and the mother explains that they've come from Kyiv so they did not need to rush to bomb shelters anymore. Lviv is so far from the front line, it's largely escaped Russia's attacks. But no – tonight the Russians are targeting a power station in the suburbs of Lviv, so we're all down here in the dark, the only light coming from the phones everyone's looking at.

What moves me is that the two-year-old isn't restless and complaining – he's so good, even though it's the middle of the night. He chats away to his mother and father, whoever takes turns holding him. I wonder how long this good-natured banter can continue. It goes on hour after hour. Various people fall asleep in the bunker, and the little boy's behaviour remains polite and chirpy.

As I look at this family, I think how unfair all this is – that Putin, with his billions and his staff of hundreds who pander to his every need, is probably fast asleep in his luxury, ultra-fortified dacha outside Moscow or in one of his underground security bunkers beneath his various hideouts. His three or four body doubles are probably also asleep – they've done their work acting as decoys for anyone who wants to kill the Russian leader. Meanwhile Ukrainians struggle with lack of sleep and dislocation. And the people in this bunker are among the lucky ones; they haven't fled the country as refugees, and they are still alive.

In this moment, I realise that this has become the new normal. This is how it is for Ukrainians and will be for the indefinite future. Across the country, night after night, Putin's army causes disruption and anguish. The night-time sirens bring a fear far beyond what is logical. Mathematically, the chance of a person in a city the size of Kyiv or Lviv being hit by a missile, drone or falling debris is small. But the longer you're in Ukraine, the more you hear stories of people who have been killed or injured by missiles or, more commonly, by metal debris falling from the sky after a Russian missile is exploded by the army's US-supported air defence system. In Ukraine, the sirens therefore play with your mind. They are certainly playing with mine.

Like many Ukrainians, whenever I find myself lying in the darkness as an air-raid siren rings out, I consider the possibility of a missile hitting the building I'm in. Am I more vulnerable being on the twelfth floor of a hotel or the second? Is there a danger going to a bunker? What if the building collapses and those of us in a bunker are buried? I've begun thinking about what I will do if I'm trapped underneath rubble. I decide that the first thing I'll do is to turn off my phone. That may sound irrational, but my logic is that it would take a day or two for search and rescue people to begin checking under the rubble and that *this* would be the time you'd want to have some battery left on your phone, not the first few chaotic hours. Ukrainians tell me that they also have these sorts of catastrophic and often irrational thoughts, usually in the middle of the night.

War plays with your mind. This is a key weapon in Putin's assault on Ukraine – he's getting value for money. The fear each missile or drone creates has a psychological multiplier effect way beyond the financial cost of each weapon. Putin is getting a fear dividend on his investment. Vladimir Putin is, more than anything else, a creature of the notorious Soviet secret service, the KGB, where fear is one of the major weapons in the operational toolkit.

On the Ukrainian side, they've also worked out a way to waste Russian resources in this war of attrition. Each day across the country, young people go around gathering old or broken parts of cannons or anti-aircraft machines and assembling them. From the height of Russian satellites and drones they look real, which causes Russian soldiers to expend artillery shells (and valuable time and brainpower) trying to hit them. The young people delight in the fact that Russian soldiers are using expensive supplies trying to hit useless installations.

This same tragic game also works against them. Ukrainians have learnt to dread the sound of drones outside their apartments, a tyranny of fear that is such an important part of Putin's war of mental attrition. One woman told me that drones, missiles and air sirens had given her a serious anxiety condition. She became jumpy – neighbours moving furniture in a nearby apartment would make her start with fear – and found it hard to sleep. This war fatigues the entire nation. Getting on trains in the underground metro or on buses, I notice how exhausted Ukrainians are. I've never seen as many people falling asleep on public transport as during my time in Ukraine. It made me sad to see it. And angry.

But I had also never seen such determination. 'We may be tired, but we are also determined to get out of bed each morning and get to work,' one woman tells me. 'Even if we haven't had much sleep, getting out of bed and getting on with our day is a victory over Putin.'

*

What disturbs me most about the scene in this bunker in Lviv isn't the horror of war: it's the normalcy of it. Even though Ukraine's air defence has now become world-class – thanks in part to Patriot systems donated by the US, Germany and the Netherlands – the public still has to take cover at all hours of the day and night. Even though most missiles and drones are shot down, the danger from falling debris cannot be eliminated, so parents like those with me in the bunker feel they have no choice but to take their children from their beds and bring them to these shelters. As the mother in that Lviv bunker tells me, 'If it was just me and my husband, we probably wouldn't bother, but with children you feel you cannot take a chance.'

As I sit in the half-light of this hotel bunker, I think how the man ultimately responsible for protecting this family is another family man – Volodymyr Zelensky, who also has two young children. The Ukrainian president is not just charged with protecting them but also trying to end this tragic reality. The more I speak to Ukrainians, the more I realise that they, too, are placing their hopes in their army and Zelensky, surely a burden almost impossible to bear.

This book digs into the mindset of Zelensky – the leader of this people's army – as well as Putin and his cronies. It also touches on the fascinating geopolitics swirling around this war, including the role of Donald Trump and American politics. When Trump was elected in 2016, Russia's parliament, the Duma, broke into applause, thrilled with this wonderful result for Putin and Russia. Trump's re-election in 2024 will be decisive in terms of the future of Ukraine. In Ukraine I found that before that 2024 election many military and government people, as well as ordinary citizens, were more focused on Washington and who would win the American election than they were on Moscow. If the world grows tired of this conflict and decides it is up to the Russians and Ukrainians to work it all out, then the sort of scene in this bunker tonight would be Putin's victory.

Underlying the Ukraine war is a generational divide. Putin and his inner circle are men in their seventies from an era and KGB culture in which the fall of the Soviet Union was the defining event of their lives. Zelensky, a man in his mid-forties, campaigned for office by spending time with young people at concerts, cafés and sporting events. Putin's war is about the past, trying to recapture historic glory and territory. Zelensky's war is about the future, trying to repel an invader so Ukraine can exist as a sovereign country independent of its powerful neighbour.

If they don't fight, either at the front line or behind the scenes, Ukrainians in their twenties and thirties feel they may not have a future. This is a powerful motivator.

That is why this war is unlike anything I have covered before. There are soldiers dug into trenches along the 1200-kilometre front line, but the majority of people fighting in Ukraine are nowhere near it. There's a whole other war going on across the country. It's being fought in backyards, where people are testing drones while children run excitedly after them. It's being fought in cafés and bars, where baristas and bartenders make phone calls between serving customers about the deliveries they're planning to make to the front on their days off. It's being fought by journalists in their twenties who, during the day, confront politicians about things they've done or said but come night-time join together to try to hack Russian computers. It's being fought by university lecturers who sit in the trenches of the Donbas and determinedly deliver their lectures online. Overall, it's being fought by Ukrainians who have asked themselves what they can contribute to a war with Russia.

Winston Churchill famously said of the Nazis, 'We shall fight on the beaches … we shall never surrender.'[3] If I could summarise the mood of Ukrainians it would be: we will fight them in the factories and in the university lecture halls. We will fight them in the research laboratories and the boardrooms where we will raise money. We will fight them in our local parks and in our classrooms. We will fight them in our basements where we will convert drones once used by farmers to fertilise their crops into birds of death carrying explosives. We will fight them in our minds, our hearts and our backyards. And even if Russian troops move into Kyiv, we will never surrender.

CHAPTER 1

Day zero

FOR VASYL MYROSHNYCHENKO, 23 FEBRUARY 2022 WAS
the day before his world changed. Two weeks earlier, Ukraine's
Ministry of Foreign Affairs had chosen him to be Ukraine's next
ambassador to Australia, and the Australian government had
accepted the appointment. It was an exciting time for him and
his family, the start of a big new adventure. Now all he had to
do was bide his time in his Kyiv apartment and farewell friends,
family and colleagues while waiting for his ambassadorship to
come through.

It's funny how the mind works, the sorts of details that stay
with us in times of crisis. The thing that Myroshnychenko most
remembers about the night before Russia's invasion is ironing a
shirt for work the next day. That shirt would remain hanging

in the same spot for months as the war caused havoc in his life. Suddenly his world became about traffic queues while he tried to get his children out of Ukraine to safety, and then joining the war effort against Russia.

Like all Ukrainians, Myroshnychenko had seen the build-up of Russian troops along the border but did not believe that an invasion would happen. About 100,000 Russian troops had gathered, but Myroshnychenko remained hopeful that his country would not face the horror of an invasion by the world's fourth-largest army. He'd been comforted by a conference he'd recently attended at a Paris think-tank where the French participants had a strong view that Putin would not invade. Many Germans had the same view. Myroshnychenko thought it was unusual that the US so strongly asserted that an invasion was about to happen yet these two key NATO countries, France and Germany, clearly had doubts. 'I was pleased to hear the reassurance from the French,' Myroshnychenko said later. 'It appealed to my optimism.'

Even the Ukrainian government hoped that Putin would not cross the line. 'Let's say we received some information from our partners that Russia had prepared an invasion,' Yegor Dubinsky, the deputy minister for digital transformation, told me later. 'But, as usual, hope is stronger than threat, and we hoped that it would not happen.'

The widely held view – or hope – across Ukraine that

Russia was bluffing was shattered at 4 am on 24 February. Myroshnychenko's wife, Lina, woke him. 'Russia has invaded,' she said. The couple turned on their television and checked social media. The TV news and social media feeds were full of pictures of Russian troops crossing the border into Ukraine. There were dramatic pictures of Russian helicopters flying into Hostomel airport just outside Kyiv. News bulletins were now replete with pictures of tanks and soldiers and rockets being fired into the country's capital.

Ukraine was at war. The couple's first thought was to get their five-year-old son and eighteen-year-old daughter to safety. And with the Russians targeting the city in which they lived, safety meant leaving Ukraine.

But there was a problem: Myroshnychenko's passport was at his office in Maidan Square. Without it, he couldn't leave. Panic was already setting in to the city and he could see from his apartment that the roads were gridlocked, so he rushed to the subway. That was itself an unnerving experience. Usually that early in the morning Kyiv's underground was not crowded, but the trains and platforms were packed. 'It was different from any other subway ride I'd taken,' Myroshnychenko said. 'Everyone was rushing, trying to get somewhere, not making much eye contact. You could tell everyone was stressed.'

Back home by 8 am, the couple loaded their luggage and children into the car and began what they hoped would be their journey west to the safety of either Poland or Romania. But the roads were clogged, and by 10 pm that evening they were still in Kyiv, the main highway to the west gridlocked. Myroshnychenko realised that he should have taken the road south then west, rather than join the tens of thousands trying to drive towards Poland. 'I wasn't thinking straight,' he said. 'We were in a blur.'

Myroshnychenko remembered that some friends who had left the country two months earlier had an empty house to the south of Kyiv, near the airport at Hostomel. The road to Hostomel was relatively uncrowded, and the friends said they were welcome to stay there. Arriving late that night, Myroshnychenko and his family had a place to stay, but their choice of refuge was arguably less safe than if they had stayed in Kyiv, as one of the biggest and earliest battles was beginning at Hostomel airport, where Russia was flying in hundreds of soldiers in helicopters. The skyline resembled the famous scene from Francis Ford Coppola's classic *Apocalypse Now* where helicopters fly across the horizon. That night, as the family tried to sleep, they could hear explosions not far away. Myroshnychenko realised they had to leave urgently, so the following day they headed to his hometown, Volochysk, four hundred kilometres to the south.

That provided a safe haven for a week, but there was no certainty about how much of the country the Russians would take. He looked at the map. He could tell from social media and other reports that the border with Poland was chaotic, so he decided the best way to get his wife and children out was to go through Romania. The family drove to that border and again encountered gridlock stretching for kilometres.

Myroshnychenko left the car and walked four kilometres to the checkpoint to ascertain the prospects of getting his family through the crossing. While doing that he met a colleague who explained that if he did not need to take his car across the border, a Red Cross van was transporting people to the border in an express lane. So his wife and children got a ride in one of these vans and crossed the border, but Myroshnychenko himself did not want to leave – he wanted to help with the war effort. The only reason he'd leave would be if approval for his ambassadorship came through as he would be able to lobby for resources and weapons from Australia. So he drove back to his parents' apartment in Volochysk, which for the next few weeks became his new office.

A fluent English speaker and a partner in a communications firm, Myroshnychenko helped the Ukrainian government with their communications while he waited, joining the team that dealt with foreign and Ukrainian media. He assumed that with the chaos caused by war, his posting to Australia would be delayed indefinitely. But he was wrong – President Zelensky was determined that the government and its bureaucracies should try to function as normally as possible despite the war. So on 9 March 2022, Zelensky officially announced three new ambassadorial appointments to Canada, Egypt and Australia.

Vasyl Myroshnychenko was now Ukraine's ambassador-designate to Australia. But he still had a problem: all his clothes – including that ironed shirt and suits – were in his Kyiv apartment, which he could not access. The government had decided in the first days of the war that its advisers and officers should work from home wherever possible, particularly if those homes were outside Kyiv. This dispersed essential workers, reducing the risk of officials being killed in attacks on Kyiv. So with no suit, but a new job in Australia, Myroshnychenko finally drove to Bucharest, Romania, where he was reunited with his family.

It was a joy and relief to be back with his wife and children, but he had an important mission. He knew from his experience with the media that for Ukraine to win a war with Russia, they would need support from around the world. Living in a country such as Australia would be important given its influence with allies such as the US and UK.

With that in mind, Myroshnychenko and his family boarded a plane to Doha and then Sydney. If he thought the last few weeks had been a whirlwind, it was nothing compared to his new life. His first mission in Australia was to organise for President Zelensky to address the two houses of the Australian parliament by video. No head of state had ever given Australia a virtual address. Zelensky knew from day one that he had to fight on two fronts: the physical front line and the international stage. This was the only way to ensure that Ukraine secured funding and weapons. If Ukraine had to fight Russia on its own, it stood no chance. Without an international coalition, the country would soon no longer exist.

On 30 March 2022, members of both houses of the Australian government gave a standing ovation to the Ukrainian president as Myroshnychenko sat in the chamber watching. For a man who a week before had fled his country with barely more than the clothes on his back, this was an overwhelming moment. 'I sat there watching history,' he said. 'The first address to the joint Australian parliament by video by a foreign leader. This was a very proud moment for me and Ukraine.'

The following day, 1 April, Myroshnychenko visited Australia's governor-general to present his credentials. He was now Ukraine's ambassador to Australia. He'd made the journey through that gridlocked traffic on day zero to be his country's representative on the other side of the world. Now his task was to lobby Australia to help Ukraine win its war against Russia.

*

At exactly the time that Vasyl Myroshnychenko was ironing his shirt in Kyiv on the evening of the day before, Solomiya Khoma and an extraordinary group of Ukraine's best and brightest gathered for a drink. They met in Arsenal, a trendy part of Kyiv that is home to many of the country's powerful elite, including President Zelensky, at a bar called Piana Vyshnia, which translates into English as 'drunken cherry'.

It was a cold winter evening, but there was no rain or snow so the group decided to sit outside. The one concession to the cold night was that the entire group ordered one of Ukraine's most popular alcoholic drinks, a hot cherry schnapps known as a Vyshneva Nalyvka. Anyone sitting at a nearby table who overheard this group's conversation would have been intrigued. While many Ukrainians were convinced that Russia would not invade, this group believed quite the opposite. In fact, they talked with certainty about a Russian invasion, which they believed was likely to come the following morning.

How right they were. So what did these young people know that other Ukrainians did not?

This group was from the Ukrainian Security and Co-operation Centre, a think-tank that assists the Ukrainian government on research for various projects. For several months they'd been sending weekly reports to the Ukrainian Ministry of Defence about the situation in Russia. Like hawks, they'd been watching developments inside Russia. They'd noticed a significant increase in infrastructure development at military bases, and a stockpiling of plasma blood supplies, something a country would most likely only do if they were expecting a war or other heavy demand on blood transfusions.

As they sat that night drinking their cherry schnapps, this group had no doubt that Russia had been preparing for war. Settling into their conversation, one of the group quipped, 'This could be the last drink we have when we're not at war.'

The last report they'd sent to the Ministry of Defence, dated 10 February 2022, exactly two weeks before the invasion, was stunningly accurate. Headlined 'Analysis of readiness for further military escalation in Ukraine by the Russian Federation based on open data', it said: 'The last few days have seen aggressive statements from the law enforcement agencies of the Russian Federation in the direction of Ukraine.' It reported that the head of Russia's Foreign Intelligence Service stated publicly that Ukraine was preparing for a full-scale war in the Donbas and was 'preparing provocations'. Russian media accused Kyiv of killing more than 5500 Russian-speaking civilians in the Donbas, including children. The report noted that there was a further transfer of equipment and manpower to the border with Ukraine and the territories Russia already occupied in Crimea and the east. Presciently, the report said: 'In Russian expert circles, military expert Pavel Felgenhauer expressed the opinion that the General Staff of the Russian Federation is ready for war. The Kremlin plans to land an amphibious assault [from

Crimea] in the deep rear of Ukraine – the Odessa region, with the occupation of the south, as well as attacks from the east. The question of whether there will be a war will be decided today.'

The group's analysis was spot-on. Drawing on US intelligence and trying to head off an invasion, US National Security Adviser Jake Sullivan said on 11 February: 'The way that [Putin] has built up his forces and put them in place, along with the other indicators that we have collected through intelligence, makes it clear to us that there is a very distinct possibility that Russia will choose to act militarily, and there is reason to believe that that could happen on a reasonably swift timeframe ... Now, we can't pinpoint the day at this point, and we can't pinpoint the hour, but what we can say is that there is a credible prospect that a Russian military action would take place.'[4]

Russia had been beating the drums of war for months. Reuters news agency[5] outlined the weeks leading to the invasion. On 24 January, NATO put forces on standby and reinforced Eastern Europe with more ships and fighter jets. On 26 January, Washington responded to Russia's security demands, repeating a commitment to NATO's 'open-door' policy while offering a 'pragmatic evaluation' of Moscow's concerns.

Two days later, Russia said its demands were not addressed. Over the following two weeks, the US said it would send 3000 extra troops to NATO members Poland and Romania.

Washington and allies said they would not send troops to Ukraine but warned of severe economic sanctions if Putin took military action. On 21 February, Putin said in a TV address that Ukraine is an integral part of Russian history and has a puppet regime managed by foreign powers.

Tensions increased when Putin ordered 'peacekeeping forces' into two breakaway regions in eastern Ukraine after recognising them as independent. The following day, the US, Britain and their allies sanctioned Russian parliament members, banks and other assets in response to Putin's troop order. Germany halted the Nord Stream 2 gas pipeline project. On 23 February, Russian-backed separatist leaders asked Russia for help repelling aggression from the Ukrainian army.

For the group sipping hot cherry drinks, there was no doubt that Moscow was preparing for war, both logistically and by pumping out propaganda in the state media. The group's predictions were bolstered by international intelligence: US and British intelligence were receiving well-sourced information about Putin's planning for war, and so was the rest of the world. Normally any intelligence is kept strictly confidential, but unusually, this information was being widely dispersed by Washington and London. In retrospect, it was a smart decision. For decades, intelligence agencies had an automatic default position that all intelligence should be kept from the public, but by revealing much of the real-time intelligence they were receiving about Russia's final preparations for war, the public was better informed. This also meant key politicians among Ukraine's allies had more time to consider the support they would give Ukraine. And Russia had nowhere to hide.

Soon after, with colleague Geraldine Doogue, we would interview the head of the Australian Secret Intelligence Service (ASIS), Paul Symon, who made an intriguing comment about the US decision to release what once would have been regarded as highly classified information. Saying that he saw this development as positive, Symon tells us:

The Russian invasion of Ukraine this year has signalled a shift in the way intelligence is shared with the public and other countries. I think that one of the hallmarks of the Russia–Ukraine conflict is the extent to which the US intelligence community in particular declassified intelligence. It helped European governments in particular – and the public – better think about or understand what should be an appropriate reaction to an incursion of that nature. Should we provide aid, either lethal or non-lethal aid? Should there be sanctions imposed? I think when you declassify intelligence in an appropriate way, you give the public an opportunity to really debate it and think about what's at stake here. I think what happened

in the early stages of Ukraine–Russia has probably set the
bar high for intelligence officials going forward to do what
they can to help inform not only government but the public.

Although they weren't the CIA, MI6 or ASIS, the Drunken
Cherry group may as well have been. They felt confident this
would be their final peacetime drink. And because they had
studied Russia's preparations for war, they had made their own
plan over a month ago. Each of them had packed a bag with
everything they needed to survive, and they had a plan in the
event that Russia invaded. On this night at the Piana Vyshnia
in Kyiv, they reinforced that plan, nominating an apartment
owned by one of them that would be the meeting place if war
broke out. Anyone prepared to join the 'resistance' – the word
they used – would be welcome to attend. (As it would turn out,
every one of them turned up to join.)

The next morning, just after 4 am, one of the group rang the
others with the news: Ukraine was at war. Vladimir Putin had
crossed the line in every sense. Of the 44 million Ukrainians,
this group would be one of the best organised. Because they'd
had a plan in place for a month, reinforced the night before over
drinks, they simply executed their plan: each one grabbbed their
prepacked 'go bag' and headed to the nominated apartment.

As soon as they arrived, they set up a call centre specifically
designed to assist members of the Territorial Defence, a reserves

unit within the Ukrainian army with whom they had done considerable work. 'Within the first twenty-four hours in that apartment we took ten thousand calls on our call centre,' says Solomiya Khoma, one of the members. 'We did everything – communications, organising food and water for delivery to soldiers, answering questions that soldiers or anyone else had. Over the next few days, we helped to mobilise around a hundred thousand people.'

Those early days were chaos. Few Ukrainians knew what was happening and what was likely to happen. There was panic everywhere. Daryna Povorozniuk, twenty-eight, was desperate to escape the war.[6] Six months pregnant, she said goodbye to her husband, a soldier keen to get to the front line to try to halt the Russian push, and boarded a crowded train. 'Things were dangerous,' she later told the ABC. Even though she had a ticket, the only room on the train was a small space normally reserved for two people. She squeezed into that area with seven other adults, a child and a dog. 'It was panicked in Ukraine everywhere. Knowing I was pregnant, I knew I had to leave and go somewhere safe.' For Daryna, that somewhere safe would be Australia, where a few months later she would give birth to her son, Eli, in the Mater Mothers' Hospital in South Brisbane.

Ukrainians also created their own chaos. Teams began painting over road signs pointing to different towns. They wanted to make sure that if the Russians did actually get close to Kyiv that they literally wouldn't know which way to turn. Ukraine did this to try to buy time until help from the US and other NATO countries could arrive. It's unclear, in the age of global positioning systems and satellite images, just how effective the covering of signs would be, but it's a reflection of the instant reactions of Ukrainians to defend themselves.

During my time in the country, I asked dozens of Ukrainians what it felt like to so suddenly be a country at war. Of all the interviews that I did for this book, it's the answer from Solomiya Khoma, one of the Drunken Cherry team, that is among the most memorable. Given her group was one of the few in Ukraine certain that an invasion was coming, I asked how she felt when she was woken at 4 am on 24 February with the news.

'My overwhelming emotion was relief,' she said. 'The war between Ukraine and Russia had really begun in 2014 with Russia's invasion of Crimea and parts of the east. Yet much of the commentary and reporting in the West had been that Ukraine was fighting separatists. But every Ukrainian knew from 2014 that we were fighting Russia, not a group of separatists. Now the entire world would know that Ukraine was under attack by Russia, not a group of separatists. That's why that morning I felt a strong sense of relief.'

*

Relief is certainly not the emotion that Oleksandr Pipa, Ukraine's first punk rocker, is feeling. Oleksandr lives on the top floor of an apartment on the western side of Kyiv from which he has sweeping views over the city, Hostomel airport and Bucha. He wakes about 4 am to the sound of explosions, missile fire and helicopters. It's not something he ever thought he'd see: from his large kitchen window, he's watching the beginning of the first land war in Europe since World War II.

Up until this moment on day zero, Oleksandr's life has been what one would expect of one of Ukraine's most popular musicians. Through the seventies and eighties, when Ukraine was still a part of the USSR, Oleksandr built a reputation as one of the country's most original musicians. Having gone through primary and secondary school when Ukraine was part of the Soviet Union, Russian was the language that Oleksandr heard and spoke as a child more than Ukrainian. (Though Ukrainian is the official language, both tongues are commonly spoken throughout Ukraine because of its Soviet past.) His band, Vopli Vidopliassova, therefore sung in both Ukrainian and Russian and so gained a big following in the Russian-speaking world. On their sell-out tours of Russia, fans revelled in the avant-garde music and Oleksandr's wild onstage demeanour. The band members had the sort of anti-authoritarian demeanour that years later would appeal to some Russians when Pussy Riot exhibited similar traits.

'With all the tours and gigs I did in Russia, I had a lot of friends there, rock musicians,' he reminisces. But Putin stoking hostility in Russia towards Ukrainians in the 1990s brought an end to many of Oleksandr's Russian friendships. The prevailing view pushed by the Kremlin after the end of the Soviet Union in 1991 was that 'neighbours could be either enemies or slaves,' he says. 'There is nothing in between, no friends, nothing. So we Ukrainians either surrender or fight.'

From his window, Oleksandr is watching the battle around Hostomel airport and the neighbouring suburb, Bucha. He sees helicopters and smoke from missiles. Russia is beginning its invasion with an assault on the airport, trying to secure it as Moscow's major pipeline into Ukraine. If they can take control of it, they will be able to bring large numbers of troops and supplies directly into Kyiv. Oleksandr sees Russian soldiers encountering much more resistance than they anticipated as thousands of Ukrainian soldiers rush to surround the airport to begin one of the bloodiest battles of the war. Before Ukrainian soldiers got there, Russia successfully sent in special forces in scores of helicopters. Oleksandr doesn't know it as he watches this drama unfold but Putin's advance assault teams have brought with them a list of two hundred or so prominent Ukrainians designated for assassination. Ukraine's president, Volodymyr Zelensky, is top of that kill list.

Wearing a Motorhead T-Shirt declaring 'March or Die', Oleksandr is an unlikely warrior. He's lived the sort of Bohemian anti-establishment life one would expect of a punk rocker, but as he looks out his window on that fateful morning, all his patriotic instincts kick in. He rushes straight to a checkpoint that's been set up by the Ukrainian army outside his building to help build fortifications.

Within hours, Kyiv has gone from being one of the most cosmopolitan cities in Europe to a front line against the Russian army. The horrible reality of an instant war is on display for everyone in Oleksandr's neighbourhood to see. Ambulances and civilian cars bring injured soldiers from the fighting at the airport and what becomes known as the Battle of Bucha. His neighbours realise that what their country is going to need urgently is medical clinics. Having helped to set up roadblocks, Oleksandr and his neighbours now start building a pop-up medical clinic. Within days he applies to join a Territorial Defence unit, a form of army reserves.

For Oleksandr, the first few days of the war are madness. Hundreds of people join queues to try to enlist in the army, sometimes spending days waiting. Even when air-raid sirens sound, many won't leave for a shelter – they don't want to lose their positions in the queues. Oleksandr hears that some people who are not medically fit for military service are trying to bribe recruiting officers to allow them to join.

From his kitchen, Oleksandr can see the road from Kyiv to the west. He can see evidence of fighting about fifteen kilometres away – Ukrainian troops firing artillery at the Russians – and a Russian missile hits a building only five hundred metres from his home. As a musician, Oleksandr's hearing is acutely trained to sound. He can tell where the Russian missiles are coming from. He says it's terrifying.

Russian soldiers are on the outskirts of Kyiv and trying to push into the centre. Oleksandr's application for the army's Territorial Defence Forces is accepted. He's assigned to reinforce a checkpoint on the highway from his neighbourhood to Bucha, where fighting is intensifying.

Oleksandr sees the invader as 'the Russian bear'. That bear, he says, has lost its balance, 'and the whole world knows that a powerful, dreadful state is about to collapse because of the efforts of millions of Ukrainians and the civilised world.'

We're intrigued about his metaphor of the teetering Russian bear. Would he like to see the bear dead?

He pauses. 'I would like to see the bear in a cage.'

Sylvie and I spent two fascinating evenings with Oleksandr, the first in his apartment where he's built a recording studio. He's meticulously soundproofed it, something his neighbours no doubt appreciate when he is singing and playing electric guitar at full blast through the midnight hours. Would he play something for us? He smiles and says of course, turning on his amplifier to belt out a song.

L'amour est un oiseau rebelle

Que nul ne peut apprivoiser,

Et c'est bien en vain qu'on l'appelle,

S'il lui convient de refuser;

Rien n'y fait, menace ou prière,

L'un parle bien, l'autre se tait;

Et c'est l'autre que je préfère,

Il n'a rien dit, mais il me plaît.

L'amour est enfant de bohème,

Il n'a jamais, jamais connu de loi,

Si tu ne m'aimes pas, je t'aime,

Si je t'aime, prends garde à toi !

Si tu ne m'aimes pas,

Si tu ne m'aimes pas, je t'aime !

Mais si je t'aime, si je t'aime,

Prends garde à toi!

Love is a rebellious bird

That none can tame,

And it is quite in vain that one calls it,

If it suits it to refuse;

Nothing to be done, threat or plea.

The one talks well, the other is silent;

And it's the other that I prefer,

He said nothing, but he pleases me.

Love is a gypsy child,

It has never, never known a law,

If you don't love me, I love you,

If I love you, be on your guard!

If you don't love me,

If you don't love me, then I love you!

But if I love you, if I love you,

Be on your guard!

*

An aria from Georges Bizet's 1875 opera *Carmen* isn't what you would expect from one of Ukraine's most notorious punk rockers, but then again, not much of what is happening inside the country feels normal anymore. Other people's songs are all Oleksandr has these days as, from the moment of the invasion, he's been unable to write any music. 'A small secret,' he says, leaning over his cluttered kitchen table as if he's about to tell a matter of state 'Creative people are different. Some can go on with music when there is a war, some cannot. I cannot feel inspired to write music when there is a war. Not because it's bad – people should continue with music, they should continue playing gigs and painters should continue making exhibitions – but I can't, so I decided to do what I can, something related to war.'

Today Oleksandr is pottering around his apartment in Kyiv among guitars, speakers and cat food: 'I might not look like someone at war,' he says, 'but I feel everything I do is war-related. I do nothing else.'

As we find across Ukraine, Oleksandr immediately swings from his day job to war mode. Now aged fifty-eight, as a forty-year music veteran he spent most of his life being antiwar. And yet now he works on the war effort every evening. 'There is historical evidence that artists, musicians and writers were against war. That's normal because war is bad,' he explains. 'The exception is when your motherland is under attack … You cannot be antiwar when your country is under attack.'

Oleksandr wants to talk about what it was like watching the battle of Bucha from his window. 'What happened in Bucha is just the proof we are right,' he explains. 'We have to fight, otherwise there will be genocide.' The international media portrayed Bucha as a town that had been decimated by particularly brutal behaviour by Russian soldiers – many people alleged war crimes on a major scale. It was pictures of Bucha that galvanised opinion around the world against the Russians, streets littered with bodies of Ukrainian civilians.

But the perspective for Ukrainians was very different. For them, it's an outer suburb of Kyiv. For them, the atrocities committed in Bucha were atrocities being committed in their very capital. 'Bucha is twenty kilometres from here, visible from this kitchen window. It's not something abstract – it's a town I have been to a dozen times, and it's very peaceful.' He has friends there who live in picturesque little houses in the forest. 'And then some kind of monster came along and stabbed and trampled everything.' Oleksandr realises that he has personal feelings about it because it's close to him, but he is glad that the international stage has paid attention too.

He describes how his close friend's parents spent a couple of weeks underground in Bucha after the invasion, while outside people were being killed in the streets. They had no mobile phone connection, no water, no food. 'This was happening in the twenty-first century, just around the corner from where I live,' he says. 'For us, it was proof that we had to fight and win, otherwise the whole country would become a huge Bucha.'

*

If there's one symbol of Russia's atrocities in the early days of the war it's Bucha. Before being pushed out, Russian soldiers entered and carried out all sorts of atrocities over the course of thirty-two days. Photographs of those atrocities went viral and horrified the world. The pictures of dead Ukrainians strewn along the streets did more to galvanise public opinion against Russia than anything else, leading to a surge of international funding and support for Ukraine.

If there's one person who personifies Bucha it's Viktor Barkholenko. Born in Bucha, he was already something of a hero in Ukraine before the war for his tireless crusade against corruption, one of the things that Ukraine was best known for. Viktor would publish the names of public figures he believed were corrupt and details of the corruption for which he alleged they were responsible. He would publish the names of municipal officials who he believed were taking bribes in return for council approvals.

When we meet with him, Viktor picks up his phone and shows us documents that he says are evidence of various municipal officials being corrupt. He's made many enemies. Whether it was corruption at local, state or national levels, Viktor Barkholenko was on the case.

Viktor says in Ukraine the people have two main enemies: one is external, Vladimir Putin, and the other is home-grown, corruption. 'All Ukrainians for the last few years have realised the danger of this external enemy and have united to fight this enemy,' he says. 'I have been fighting the internal enemy for a very long time, and I have been through a lot of shit while fighting this enemy. I am still fighting this enemy.'

But on 24 February, war came to the town he loved. His attention went from corruption to war and how to help his neighbours, friends and family survive one of the most powerful armies in the world. 'When the war started, we were expecting that something would happen, but we did not expect it so soon,' he says. 'And we did not expect it to start here, but when it started, we found ourselves in the middle of fighting.'

After driving for an hour or so from Kyiv, Sylvie and I meet Viktor in his home in Bucha. Ukrainians have told us that to understand what life was like during Russia's month long occupation of Bucha we should meet Viktor. He greets us at his front gate like long-lost friends and begins by taking us on a tour of his large garden. He shows us the section of his fence filled with bullet holes and shrapnel marks from when the Russians came into his street. He shows us the bomb craters near his house and other bullets through neighbours' fences. He takes us a couple of streets away to show us where his friend was shot by the Russians under an old oak tree. 'Just there,' he says. 'They shot my friend in that very spot.' His friend's body lay under the tree for ten days as the Russians did not allow anyone to bury him.

Viktor then invites us to sit on the porch at the back of his house and drink some of his homemade whiskey. The porch is covered with old shells from Russian tanks that Viktor has turned into flowerpots. He says he takes delight in turning something intended to kill into something of beauty with flowers and plants. As we sip his whiskey – strong and smooth – he explains how the Russians who took over his house after he fled drank some of his oldest and best homemade blends.

On the first day of the invasion, Viktor says the sky was completely controlled by Russian fighter jets. 'Some terrible things started to happen.' One of those terrible things was the killing of a friend by a Russian missile. Viktor shows us pictures of his dead friend devastated by explosives. When Viktor heard the news of his friend's death, he rushed to their home to pick up his friend's family and bring them to his place, hoping that would be safer.

In the early days after the invasion, Viktor would drive around his neighbourhood looking to see whether anyone needed help. They had no electricity or water. But on 3 March, Russian soldiers entered the town, and driving around was impossible. 'We stayed in our house,' he says, 'and all we could do was go from garden to garden to our neighbours through our back fences, so that we weren't on the street.'

It appears the Russians had two strategic aims in Bucha. The first was to take the town street by street to give them a base from which to make a push into Kyiv. The second was to put such fear into Ukrainians that they would flee as Russian soldiers approached, making it easier to achieve their first aim. To that end, they are reported to have killed thirty six people in one street alone: Yablonska Street.

The Russians came within a few hundred metres of Viktor's house. He feared for his life for two reasons: firstly, he worried that his high profile might make the Russians think that they had some sort of 'prize', but secondly, he also worried that various powerful people in Bucha who he had campaigned against over alleged corruption could use the war as an excuse to kill him. 'I worried that some local opponents might try to kill me and make it look like war,' he says. 'So I had to flee and put all my most necessary things in my backpack and cross a small river close to Irpin.'

Viktor knew that the Ukrainian army had set up a checkpoint on the other side of the river. His aim was to get to that so he had some protection from the Russian army, which he could tell was advancing. But as he got close, he realised the checkpoint had been abandoned. He thought that if he tried to cross the bridge, the Ukrainian soldiers might think he was part of the Russian advance and open fire on him. He then thought it might be safest to go under the bridge but worried that as the Ukrainian army had retreated, they may have left mines under the bridge to make the Russian advance more dangerous. He finally decided that the risk of getting shot crossing the bridge was probably lower than the risk of going under, a decision justified later when he spoke to Ukrainian soldiers, who confirmed that they had indeed mined underneath.

The question remains: why did the Russians behave so appallingly in Bucha? Viktor thinks it's because they were envious of what they saw around them. 'They were always talking about how well people live around Bucha, how we have nice houses, good gardens,' he says. '"Why is it so nice here?" they would ask themselves.' After observing them for weeks, Viktor reckoned they were jealous of Ukraine's clean and comfortable houses; Russians, according to Viktor, are used to living in much less comfort and beauty. And when you combine that jealousy with the town's extraordinary resistance, you end up with a bloodbath. 'They expected to be victorious in a few days, but they were stopped here and pushed out,' he says. 'They were upset and angry, and they put this anger against us, the people.'

*

The residents of Bucha suffered through a war starting on their doorstep, but for Anastasiia Lebedenko it started 1600 kilometres away.

Sylvie and I meet the 22-year-old on a brilliant, sunny afternoon as she sits in the courtyard of a café in Kyiv. She's taking a break from her work as both a translator and writer. For Anastasiia, day zero was a very different experience – she was overseas when she found out her country had been invaded.

She and her boyfriend were in Italy staying with a friend when early one morning, her friend woke up and was circling around the apartment. 'I was thinking, "Why did he get up so early?"' she remembers. 'And he said, "The war has begun."'

With those four words, Anastasiia's life changed. 'Nothing would be the same after that phrase,' she says. 'Right now there is the life before the twenty-fourth of February and the life after.' From Italy she called her mother, who said she was hiding in her walk-in wardrobe, which was the safest place in the apartment during the explosions. Her mother tried to insist to her that everything would be okay. 'But nothing was going to be okay now,' Anastasia says. 'I don't know how you can say that.' She lived in a dissociated state for those early days, hardly sleeping. 'It was like adrenalin was filling my whole body for days. I could not relax, I could not detach from my phone.'

Her partner had been overseas in 2014 when Russian soldiers took parts of eastern Ukraine, and he was concerned about how quickly things had deteriorated back then. Sensing the Russians were about to do it again – this time marching unimpeded on Kyiv – he wanted to return to Ukraine. After days of monitoring the drama back home and talking to anxious friends and family members, Anastasiia and her boyfriend decided to cut short their European holiday and return home.

'We chose to come back to Ukraine, even though I could live abroad,' she says. She does her translation work remotely, so it doesn't matter where she is based. But despite the risk, she still chose to move back to Kyiv. 'There is no-one who can make these decisions for me – whether to stay, whether to emigrate, whether to move. There are so many questions, and as there may not be tomorrow, every second is precious and I have to use it.'

Anastasiia says Putin and his regime seriously misjudged Ukrainians. 'I bet they thought it would be easy,' she says. And she also thinks many other countries underestimated them too. 'They thought it would be three days and over this time,' she quips. 'The most essential thing is that people thought we lived next to Russia and were part of that culture, but in fact we exist as an antithesis to it. We exist in opposition to it, and it showed.'

With the invasion of Ukraine on 24 February also came something dramatic: a rebirth of the Ukrainian identity. Just as Gallipoli is mythically referred to as Australia's baptism by fire, Anastasiia says the war in Ukraine has given her a new understanding of what it means to be Ukrainian. Growing up, she had felt submersed in Russian culture as a result of the 'propaganda of all those years'. Anastasiia says she was taught to think that Ukrainians and Russians are very similar, but now she has realised their culture is very different. 'Before this war I did not have much awareness of what nationality means or what my culture is,' she says, 'and suddenly I have this huge legacy, this huge background behind me. It means a lot to realise who you are, where you are from and what it means. Suddenly I am Ukrainian.'

Anastasiia feels that she has already learnt a lot about herself from the war. She says that realising your national identity and what it means is a strange and empowering feeling in the current globalised world. 'I am Ukrainian, and this is my strength and this is where I come from and this is what empowers me,' she explains like a mantra. 'And it's not tying me down – it is moving me forward in so many ways … I am discovering my own culture at the age of twenty-two and it is a whole new journey, a whole new world I have not seen.'

Ukraine's war with Russia unleashed previously untapped energy. It rallied the country behind Ukraine's identity, language and flag. And for many individuals, it drew on a power source and determination that many did not realise they had.

This was just getting started. And it was about to produce some extraordinary personal stories.

CHAPTER 2

A citizen army

IT'S 14 OCTOBER 2022, AND IN A FOREST ALONG THE
front line, something remarkable is happening. A woman
in a white wedding dress with an army jacket over it stands
with a man in a Ukrainian army uniform complete with gun.
While Ukrainian troops keep a lookout for Russian soldiers,
others stand alongside the couple for the wedding ceremony.
Ukraine's 'Joan of Arc' – one of the army's most feared
snipers – is getting married.

Evgeniya Emerald has put down her gun with its telescopic
lens to marry Yevgeny Stipanyuk, a soldier she met and fell in
love with at the beginning of the war. Their wedding day, she
writes on Instagram, is 'a perfect day'.

I could not imagine a more ideal wedding! Today I
officially became the wife of a military man. It happened
on the front line and the general of the Armed Forces
of Ukraine conducted the ceremony … I want to
congratulate all the defenders. Glory to the Heroes! I also
congratulate my beloved, because today it's his birthday.
Now he will definitely never forget the date of his wedding.

Evgeniya makes the point on her Instagram that, fighting on
the front line, you understand that every day could be your last.
'And we don't want to postpone life for later.'

Evgeniya's story typifies a mantra – almost a religious
conviction – that now runs through Ukrainian society: that each
person should parlay whatever skills they have into the war effort.
Evgeniya learnt to shoot on hunting trips with her father when
she was nine. As a teenager, shooting became a hobby. Before the
war, Evgeniya had worked in a jewellery shop, but when Russia's
full invasion happened, she asked herself what she could do for
the army. She had a very valuable skill: marksmanship. With no
previous military experience, she became one of Ukraine's best
shooters in an elite unit – a fearsome sniper on the front line.
Russian soldiers learnt that if they came within a kilometre of
Evgeniya, they did so at their peril.

Soon after marrying, Evgeniya became pregnant. She
couldn't stay at the front so she thought about what other kinds

of contributions she could make back in Kyiv. She began to help a small group of women who were making army uniforms and flak jackets suitable for women. Given eight per cent of the army are women, making suitable army gear is vital for both their comfort and safety.

To the world, the image of Ukraine at war is soldiers in the trenches of the Donbas. But the most striking thing about our time in Ukraine was the way the war effort infuses itself into the entire community; almost every person you meet is involved one way or another in the war against Russia. The only way Ukraine can win a war against a bigger and better resourced enemy is for millions of its citizens to draw on their various skill sets. And as I discovered, those everyday skills have emerged as useful in the most creative ways.

*

Before I went to Ukraine, 'war effort' meant hardware, tanks, artillery and jets. In Ukraine I learnt a very different concept: the war effort was a woman sitting on her porch sewing protection for her soldiers. I've never seen a population as committed to a war effort as in Ukraine. Almost everyone you speak to has taken upon themselves a role. When the word went out that many soldiers were going to the front line without any protection, women came out of retirement to sew flak jackets and other supplies. You often see them sitting on their front porches with a cup of tea on warm evenings, knitting clothes for the front line. Musicians and DJs organise the collection of metal pieces to be inserted into body armour. They often say that Russia is fighting not just against the Ukrainian army but against the entire Ukrainian people. Young people joined the 'keyboard army', attacking Russian computer servers to prevent the sending of propaganda and creating havoc in Russian military communications.

Yet despite this massive movement underwriting the war effort, it has not been widely covered. I'd often heard the term 'war effort', but I'd never seen it up close like this.

From 24 February 2022, people rushed to defend their country. There were queues to donate blood from the very first morning and even bigger queues of people of all ages to join the army. In small villages, people with hunting rifles came together to co-ordinate the movement of supplies to the front line. Others collected bottles and materials for homemade explosives. Young engineering students helped in the construction of pop-up medical centres. Local restaurants made bread and simple food for soldiers and civilian refugees. The whole population understood what was at stake and stood up to assist however they could.

Instead of fighting, other experts used their knowledge to rebuild what had been lost. The prominent Ukrainian architect Slava Balbek, for example, began a project designing affordable, easily constructed modular homes for internally displaced people. Next he helped to develop a system that would assist in the rebuilding of ruined houses in villages. Someone whose home has been destroyed by Russian bombing can enter its parameters on a website that designs a replacement and exports the blueprint, which can then be handed to a builder. Architectural regulations vary regionally, so the website even includes the particular building codes and rules of each. It makes rebuilding destroyed houses and apartments much easier and quicker and is an extraordinary service that has grown out of this war.

Ukraine began taking people to the front line in waves. The first wave was made up of those with combat or other military experience. Volunteers without military experience went to dig trenches, while others helped to establish medical stations for the dispensing of pain medication and emergency care. At major intersections, locals used bulldozers to push destroyed cars, trucks and other obstacles into place to slow advancing Russian tanks. Thousands of Ukrainians armed only with their country's flag tried to block Russian tanks at the entrance to the city of Enerhodar, where the nuclear plant of Zaporizhzhia is situated. They sang the Ukrainian national anthem as they stood in front of oncoming tanks, and young people posted images of the actions on Youtube, Instagram and TikTok to keep morale high.

This immediate and reflexive 'people's army' was designed to buy time for Ukraine until its army could get into place and enlist tens of thousands of others. Ashot Arushanov is one of the more colourful of this people's army. The message on the T-shirt he wears under his bikie's leather jacket gives a clue that he's not one to hide his opinions: *Sex is cool but Putin's death is better!*

Ashot is a bikie from central casting. In Ukraine he's become legendary as the leader of an annual motorbike event. 'It's the largest bikie festival in the world,' he tells us within minutes of meeting. Sylvie and I meet him in a far outer suburb of Kyiv. After showing us one of his motorbikes, he takes us to the basement of his high-rise apartment building where he and another resident store supplies donated for the war effort. It's jam-packed with jumpers, jeans, T-shirts, sticky tape, serviettes, tins of tomatoes and flour – most of that will be heading to the front line. There's another section for children's items. Ukrainians know the importance of keeping the spirits and mental health of children as strong as possible during a war, so in this corner we find animal-shaped biscuits, baby car seats, children's books, small bicycles and all sorts of toys. Ashot will organise for some of his fellow bikies to take the food, water and other goods to the front line.

But that's not the only way Ashot is helping. He and his comrades repair old donated motorbikes and take them to the front, where some soldiers prefer them over traditional vehicles;

'bikie units' have the ability to move quickly to places the army jeeps cannot.

The bikie soldiers work closely with fighters from the Azov Brigade, who are some of the toughest of Ukraine's soldiers. Before the war, the Azov Brigade was a volunteer militia with close links to far-right and neo-Nazi groups in Ukraine. They were seen by many Ukrainians as dangerous hooligans. But upon the Russian invasion, the militia became a feared fighting unit integrated into the Ukrainian National Guard. The vision of this crew of heavily armed vanguards charging towards them on a fleet of motorbikes would surely strike fear into any Russian soldier.

From mechanics turning the front line into a scene from *Mad Max* to architects helping to rebuild bombed-out homes, every Ukrainian is contributing in the best way they know how. And this is never more apparent than in the jewel of the country's crown, Kyiv.

*

It was only when I drove into Kyiv for the first time that I truly understood this war. What was most striking on this first drive was just how close the Russian army got to the capital – the number of damaged and destroyed buildings on its outskirts was extraordinary. The Russian army had taken over many of the suburbs of Kyiv. They were at the gates of the city. Imagine an army pushing into the outskirts of Paris, or missile craters in the sandy Northern Beaches of Sydney. Vladimir Putin had wanted to take the capital within three days, and driving into Kyiv, you can see how extraordinarily close he came to achieving that aim. It would have changed the course of history and redrawn the map of Europe by essentially extinguishing Ukraine as a sovereign nation.

When you arrive in the city centre, another thing strikes you: the make-up of its population. After Russia invaded, millions of people fled Kyiv, primarily women and children. In neighbouring countries, particularly Poland, where most of the Ukrainian refugees went, the demographics changed dramatically, swelling the ranks of women and children.

When the war started, Ukraine introduced martial law. Since then, men between eighteen and sixty have not been allowed to leave; they are expected to stay and be ready to be called to the front line. But even though they are kept in the country by government decree, the reality is that most men I spoke to *wanted* to stay and defend their country. In fact, I was astounded by the enthusiasm of men wanting to join the army. I often saw them standing in long queues to enlist. As Russia began targeting Kyiv with Iranian-made drones in November 2022, whenever an air-raid siren sounded, most residents would move to bomb shelters, usually basements or underground metro stations. But often men remained defiantly in the queues, not wanting to lose their positions. They were prepared to risk their lives to be able to go to the front line – and once there, risk their lives for a second time.

They weren't alone. Many of the women and children who decided to remain at home made thousands of Molotov cocktails, often in the public squares of villages or in homes that had been turned into explosive-making factories. Children in many villages search for soft drink bottles to bring to the main square to be made into mini bombs. Often these Molotovs are thrown into the air vents of Russian tanks. If made and launched correctly, they can cause an explosion inside the tank, often causing fatalities.

This attitude reveals why Putin will find it hard to win this war. He can inflict untold misery on Ukraine – which he did. He can destroy families, killing parents or children or both – which he did. He can occupy Crimea – which he did. He can occupy significant parts of the Donbas in the east – which he did. He can commit war crimes by targeting residential buildings and other civilian targets. But he will find it extremely difficult to win. The more he attacks, the more Ukrainians vow that they will never surrender.

There are three key factors to consider when trying to understand Vladimir Putin's motivations. Firstly, he learnt his craft and modus operandi in Russia's intelligence service, the

KGB, one of the most ruthless spy agencies in history. Secondly, he has built a circle of advisers and security officers around him who are either former KGB or of the same mindset. And thirdly, the collapse of the Soviet Union was the defining event of his adulthood, something seen by the KGB as a complete failure of Russian leadership. Putin therefore wants to return Russia to the grand Soviet empire that he was brought up believing in, reinstituting the old world order. Taking back Ukraine is key to that vision.

But even if Putin prevailed militarily, he would never win the hearts and minds of Ukrainians. It would be an ugly occupation, much as Israel's occupation of the Palestinian territories is an ugly occupation that over time requires more and more violence to enforce. The more Putin attacks, the more determined the 44 million Ukrainians become.

In this way, the Ukraine war is clear-cut. The Russian invasion in February 2022 was just that: an invasion. Ukraine was not and is not disputed territory. Even Vladimir Putin and the hard-line nationalists around him who yearn for the old empire cannot dispute that Ukraine became an independent country after the fall of the Soviet Union. But that's not stopping them. In Russian military minds, it's not about disputing modern boundaries but rather reinstituting an old map. They have a burning anger that the once-powerful Soviet Union has been broken up, leaving a significantly diminished Russia; to vary a

Donald Trumpism, they want to 'make Russia great again'. It's worth noting that Putin himself has said that 'Russia's border does not end anywhere'.[7]

In one way, Ukraine was fortunate that Putin had convinced himself that there would be little resistance and that the Russian army would be able to march triumphantly and quickly into Kyiv. This was Putin's first major miscalculation. Former Australian army intelligence officer David Robinson told me that one of the first things that an army officer learns at military college is the force ratios required to win battles. He says that both when an army is conducting offensive attacks and when it's defending against them, it needs a three-to-one advantage to have a chance. This is taught as normal doctrine at West Point, one of the most famous military colleges in the US, and the Royal Military College in Canberra. But in a city, Robinson says, those numbers go up significantly. Instead of three-to-one, it increases to five-to-one or more.

'What confused a lot of military analysts,' says Robinson, 'is that Putin attacked with a one-to-one force ratio – Russia had the same number of soldiers as Ukraine had.' At the time of the invasion, Ukraine had a standing army of approximately 250,000, which is the same number of soldiers Putin sent in. On the ratios generally accepted by military strategists, if he wanted to take Kyiv he should have sent 1.25 million. But because he was so convinced that the Ukrainian army couldn't defend the capital, he only sent a fraction of the 3.57 million soldiers in the Russian Army.

The nature of this war shapes the way Ukrainians react to it. There's an undeniable David and Goliath element to all this. Ukraine's government likes to play this up; it's part of its international narrative when trying to convince countries around the world to contribute arms and other assistance. But just because a country or government uses something as part of its narrative or propaganda doesn't mean that it's not true. When Russia launched the invasion, its military was unquestionably more formidable than Ukraine's. But as the war went on, this differential reduced significantly to the point where, all things considered, Ukraine's army is a close match to Russia's in resource terms when pumped up by the US and other NATO countries.

I've travelled widely in my time as a journalist and covered many conflicts, but I've never seen a people more proud of their army than Ukrainians. Soldiers have a special place here. When they walk into a shop, others will insist they be served ahead of them. When they join a queue at a train station, they will be shepherded to the front of the line. People are proud to say that their sibling or child or partner is in the army. They're even prouder to say that they're at the front line, or the 'zero line' as Ukrainians call it.

This was not the first time that Ukrainians had rallied to protect their democracy. In February 2014, hundreds of thousands gathered in Maidan Square in the centre of Kyiv to protest their pro-Russian president Viktor Yanukovych. The government attacked the protesters, the most violent response to protests since the end of the Soviet Union. After five days, the European Union brokered a truce by engineering a unity government, and Yanukovych fled to Russia. The 'Maidan Revolution' taught Ukrainians how to mobilise a civilian army at short notice, and less than a decade later, their muscle memory kicked back into gear.

*

It was the moment Max Stukalo looked at his sleeping son that he decided to go to war. It was early morning on 24 February 2022, and he was in his apartment in Kyiv. He saw something he never believed he'd see through his large windows: Russian missiles being fired into Ukraine's capital.

Until that moment, Max had had a successful corporate career as a brand manager. But listening to the news as he watched the Russian attacks, Max made a decision: he would quit his corporate job and join the Ukrainian army. The next day, he and his brother went to the army recruitment office. Neither told their wives; they wanted to keep it to themselves until they'd enlisted.

A few hours later, with their enlistment papers stamped, they returned to their homes with the news. The army had given the brothers only one day to prepare. They packed whatever clothes they needed. It was particularly difficult when Max's son asked him, 'Are Russians going to kill you?'

'Our wives cried all night,' says Max, 'but they understood that we could not do anything else. They made us a good dinner, and in the early morning we went.'

Everywhere you go in Ukraine there are stories of people dropping everything on that fateful day and joining an extraordinary effort to fight in Europe's deadliest conflict since World War II. Although Max had never before served in the army, he had done some military training programs at university. In the frenzy of a country under attack, that was enough for the Ukrainian military command – they asked him to use his leadership skills and be a unit commander.

But a sudden leadership role in the military brought its own challenges. As commander, it was his grim duty to venture into the 'grey zone' of the front line, the area between Ukrainian and Russian troops, to count and identify dead Russian soldiers. The military hierarchy asked Max and other commanders to do this so that they had an estimate, albeit a very imprecise one, of the number of Russian casualties. Ukrainian drone photographs and US satellite imagery showed the number of troops being deployed, but having a sense of the number of Russians being killed was of strategic value in helping the Ukrainian military planners know which parts of the front line had heavy casualties and might be vulnerable.

So Max would photograph dead Russians with his phone, looking for any metal tags or other identifying information. Some of the bodies had been there for weeks or months. Max showed me the photos – some were gruesome, one showing a separated head. Others showed young men, cut down in the prime of their lives, after months of decay. All these bodies were lying alone in the snow of a remote field somewhere in Ukraine.

As we looked at these young Russian men, two things struck me: first, what a tragic and senseless loss of life this was. Second, these young men's own families probably did not have confirmation they had been killed. They had simply gone missing somewhere in Ukraine, left to decay in the snow while a former brand manager tried to position any identifying name tags before he took a photograph. I thought about the trail of sadness and unresolved questions each one of these men would have left back in their hometowns. There would be mothers, fathers, siblings and partners grieving, wondering how and where their loved one had fallen on this cruel battlefield.

These battlefields had thousands of uncollected Russian bodies. The Ukrainians prided themselves on making sure that they brought every one of their soldiers' bodies home; sometimes they collected their dead even at risk of their own lives. Several Ukrainian soldiers told me that it was a point of honour that a fellow Ukrainian's body would never be left on the battlefield. 'We know that if something happens to us, we will always be collected,' one said. While Russia claims that it also collects its dead, the thousands of uncollected bodies put lie to this. Under Russia's army regulations, if a body is not found, the government does not need to pay the family a lifelong pension.

Meanwhile, videos abound showing Ukrainian soldiers risking their lives to rescue injured colleagues. Max shows us footage from inside an army van of him driving with a soldier in the back seat with his leg blown off. Max is driving at an extraordinary speed – you can see the stress he is under from the frenzied look in his eyes – as he tries to get the injured soldier to a hospital. (He succeeded.) Max explains that if you can get someone who has had a limb blown off to a hospital while staunching the bleeding as much as possible, there is a chance they will survive.

Counting bodies was just one of the dramatic changes to Max Stukalo's life. Another was his relationship with his family. To let his loved ones know that he was still alive, whenever he got the chance he would send them a signal from his phone. But to do this he needed to leave his trench; the ironclad rule for every Ukrainian soldier was that they could not send any communications from their trenches as these could be intercepted and possibly alert Russians to their location. So to send a text, Max needed to find a location as far away as possible from the trenches to keep his fellow soldiers safe, but leaving the trench was also dangerous. To get a signal, sometimes Max would have to crawl *towards* the Russian line; sometimes he would even use their internet signal if it was stronger than his own side's. Max took a certain delight in this. 'I was stealing the Russians' wi-fi!' he quips.

To minimise the amount of time he was exposed, rather than send long messages, he would simply send the signal agreed with his family, a plus sign. As his sister Nataliia says, 'You are afraid of telephone calls, the ring, you are frightened of not getting this plus sign.' It was particularly difficult for her parents. 'When I looked at my parents with two of their sons at the front … it was the most stressful and challenging time in their lives.' Sometimes the family would go for days without hearing anything. Then there would be a ping on the mobile and they'd rush to the phone, thrilled if they saw the coded message.

Max says that without any question, the first month was the hardest. He says that in the immediate weeks after the invasion, he and his soldiers, hiding in trenches, only had rifles while the Russians had tanks. Somehow they managed to hold the line until the NATO equivalent of cavalry arrived. One NATO country after another contributed tanks, infantry-fighting vehicles, long-range missiles, rockets, mortars, military training and bullets. Thanks to these massive contributions, by the middle of 2023, Ukraine would become one of the most serious and best-equipped armies in the world. But that was not the case in February 2022. The Russians had jumped the Ukrainians, taking them by surprise.

Max says that for many Ukrainians, in the first few days it felt like they were fighting 'a war without weapons'. His soldiers were initially seriously outgunned. The Russians quickly realised that the Ukrainian soldiers did not have 'anything with big distance' to destroy their tanks, so they became bolder, driving their tanks right up to the trenches that the Ukrainians had made. His soldiers saw one Russian tank start to shoot, and once the Russians in the tank realised that the Ukrainians didn't have any heavy weapons, they approached the Ukrainians, lowered the tank's gun barrel and started firing directly into the trenches. The human stories from those frightening first days are dramatic.

At the start of the war, the Ukrainian army was also positioned in the wrong location. In the months leading up to the invasion, the Russian military had been massing on Ukraine's eastern border. Russia expert Professor Mark Edele told me that Ukraine's military command had prepared for a possible assault from the Russian-occupied regions of Donbas in the east of the country, so it had positioned the majority and best of their troops there. They had not expected the three-sided assault that Russia executed. This meant that Kyiv was relatively vulnerable.

The battle of Kyiv would last a month and could have gone either way. On the first day, Russian special forces flew into

Hostomel airport on Kyiv's outskirts and quickly moved on foot into the suburbs. 'Firefights broke out as close as four kilometres from government headquarters,' Professor Edele says.

'Zelensky, who had famously declined a "ride" out of the city by his American allies, remained to post defiant video messages to the citizens of his country. With the airborne assault on Hostomel airport suppressed and the teams of assassins eradicated, the major threat remained, however: the columns of armour moving in two groups from the north towards the city which, because of the successful deception by the Russian armed forces, was nearly defenceless: Russia had a twelve-to-one advantage in forces north of Kyiv. Things looked bleak.'

In fact, things looked extremely bleak. One commander told me that in the first two weeks of the war, seventy per cent of his platoon was killed or injured, about 380 of his 500-plus soldiers. Until Ukraine caught its military breath, this was slaughter. In the early weeks, far more Ukrainian soldiers were killed than Russians. But Ukraine put up enough of a resistance – just – to keep the Russian army at the gates of Kyiv. And then, using grit, determination and massive human sacrifice, they forced the Russians from the gates back to the Donbas where a long-term gridlock ensued. Once the two sides settled into this gridlock, more Russians than Ukrainians would die on any typical day.

The Russian army had the Ukrainian army against the wall. But what Vladimir Putin had not counted on was one of the biggest mobilisations of civilians in history – the immediate and spontaneous emergence of a huge people's army.

*

Twelve Ukrainian soldiers have come straight from one of the toughest battles of this war – the battle of Bakhmut – and are now gathering in a stable on the outskirts of Kyiv. They're greeted by Anna, a psychologist who owns and has brought along her ten horses, four dogs and two cats. Instantly, the soldiers are surrounded by the chaos, sounds and smells of animals, a wonderful change from the chaos, sounds and smells of war. The psychologist is delighted: for the soldiers, she says, the next few hours will be a much-needed 'resting and rebooting'.

Today I'm joining a program called Spirit Warrior, the creation of Anna Burago. Anna is another example of Ukrainians asking themselves what they have to offer and then how they can go about offering it. And what better gift than the warmth, adoration and healing powers of animals. Thousands of Ukrainian soldiers are returning from the front line, either permanently or for a break, with post-traumatic stress disorder (PTSD), which during World War I and II was given the catch-all label of shellshock. The trauma affecting Ukrainian soldiers and civilians more broadly will last for years, if not decades. So rather than fighting in the trenches, Anna has used her expertise as a psychologist and her adoring and energetic family of sixteen animals to try to give soldiers some relief from war.

I'm spending the day with this group of twelve paratroopers, who are among the most elite and best trained in the Ukrainian army. They've come from Bakhmut in Ukraine's east where they've been fighting in what is considered one of the bloodiest battles since the end of World War II. Both Russia and Ukraine made Bakhmut an emblematic battle, and the number of soldiers killed and injured was wildly out of proportion to its strategic significance; Russia alone is estimated to have lost more than 30,000 men. For both Putin and Zelensky, Bakhmut became a battle of pride – one side would perhaps gain fifty metres one week only to have the other side take back thirty metres the next.

It's no surprise, given how tough life is at the front line, that when these soldiers arrive, they are quiet, almost sullen. I'm introduced to them, but they're not responsive. I cannot begin to imagine the horrors they've been through. But on this glorious day, as we stand in the stable among bales of hay and the smell of horses, that brutal war begins to feel a long way away. The sounds of horses echo across the neighbourhood as the soldiers wait for the program to begin.

Anna explains to me that she created Spirit Warrior because one of the most important issues in Ukraine is helping soldiers cope with possible PTSD. As part of that recovery, she combines her traditional work as a psychologist with animal therapy.

'When PTSD is developing,' she says, 'a person gets stuck in their reality, in what can be their horrible reality. And often the person can't escape this reality. They can keep returning to that reality and feel stress.' Once soldiers have come to Anna's farm for a combination of psychotherapy, horse grooming and riding, they begin to reconnect with reality. 'It might not look much, but the person is distracted because, being on the horse, you're focused on not losing your balance,' she explains. 'The horrible reality which they can be stuck in just fades away.' The program also works with many people who have been driven from their homes because of the war. 'They're often our guests.'

Anna introduces me to the leader of these paratroopers, Commander Oleg, who asks me for security reasons not to use his surname. 'Everywhere at the front line is difficult,' he says. 'Bakhmut is the place where very intensive military actions are happening now. I would say it's a red zone, a serious one. And we are infantry, and infantry are those who are seeing enemies at three or five or six metres. That's why this program, thanks to the organisers and our command, is so good – it gives us the opportunity to have this rehabilitation after fighting in such stressful conditions.'

What happens when Commander Oleg finds himself five or six metres from a Russian soldier? 'Either the enemy finishes you or you finish the enemy,' he says matter-of-factly. He explains that pilots in a war only see the results of their attacks later, through photographs, and those operating artillery from kilometres away from their enemy only know the results of their actions through official reports. But his team of paratroopers come as close to hand-to-hand combat as modern warfare allows.

Among the close-combat enemy that these men have been fighting are not just Russian soldiers but fighters from Russia's Wagner Group. This feared private army is also hired by other nations to do their dirty work, such as by the Assad regime during the Syrian civil war, and also played a large role in African conflicts in Sudan, Libya and the Central African Republic on behalf of the Russian Government. 'Partly they're professionals,' says Commander Oleg, 'but for us they are enemies.'

Wagner doesn't operate like a normal army. For its involvement in the war in Ukraine it enlisted 40,000 convicts into its forces, often giving them minimal training before being sent into battle. These convicts – often murderers and rapists – were released from Russian prisons in return for agreeing to go to the front line where there was a high chance they would be killed. Commander Oleg says there's a distinction within Wagner between those fighters who had military experience and those who came directly from jails. During the battle of Bakhmut, ninety per cent of the 20,000 men Russia lost were former prisoners. 'Their losses show our capacity and level of training,' he says.

But today, Commander Oleg is not concentrating on 'liquidating' Wagner fighters – rather, he's pleased that the Ukrainian military is moving early to deal with PTSD and other mental health problems. He appreciates that it is happening 'straight after the fighting, not when the psychological illness has developed already,' he says. 'Animals can have a really serious influence on people.'

I meet one of Commander Oleg's young soldiers. When we shake hands, he introduces himself as 'Soldier Timothy'. After heavy combat near Bakhmut, he says he's found it difficult to relate to people. His team spent two months fighting around Bakhmut, including a month within the city itself, where fighting was at close range. He watched hundreds of fighters die – Russian, Ukrainian and Wagner mercenaries.

I say to Timothy that being in a stable surrounded by these animals must seem a world away from the horrors of Bakhmut. 'It's a huge contrast,' he says, 'not only with animals but with people.' He tells me that it's been difficult to reintegrate into normal life and speak to people, but with horses, you don't have to speak at all. 'You can communicate with animals even without words,' he says. 'And it lets you unload very much.'

Anna is standing next to Commander Oleg and Soldier Timothy, clearly proud of the program that she's created. '[The soldiers] need a recovery,' she says. 'This is about recovery, relaxation, calmness, happiness, rebooting, the most important feelings for psychology – being in the here and now.'

The first step in today's program is for the soldiers to be introduced to their horses. Then they're asked to groom them, creating a bond between soldier and horse. They feed them carrots and lettuce. Once the soldiers get comfortable with their horses, they're helped to mount them. Then they go into a riding circle. Some are more confident than others, but as I sit here watching, I notice a common response from every soldier: each soldier begins smiling immediately. Some laugh – sometimes nervously as they tentatively sit atop the horse – but the delight from all is obvious to see. It's a real joy to watch. I'm staggered by the contrast with what I saw when the soldiers arrived a few hours ago. The positive impact of these beautiful horses on these men is almost miraculous. Watching this has made me realise the emotional balm and healing power of animals.

Once the soldiers are comfortable doing the riding circle, they're asked to do stretching exercises with their arms and shoulders at the same time. It's not easy for those who are not experienced riders, so they're all focusing completely on these horses and maintaining their balance – and the death and fear of Bakhmut recedes, even if only for a few hours.

Over this session, a group dynamic of fun emerges, something they have not enjoyed together in some time. As in any large group, a couple of soldiers emerge as jokers, entertaining the others. From a group that arrived in almost sullen silence, laughter now rings out among the sounds of horses and dogs.

It's impossible to gauge exactly how much the soldiers have unloaded, but Anna says that many of the hundreds of soldiers who have been through this program find it difficult to leave the horses. 'A lot of soldiers come to us saying that they have come to a different world, it's a different reality,' she says. 'A lot of men are saying that they don't want to leave this place, they want to come back. They ask, "Can we live here with you?"'

Many soldiers find lasting benefits. Their sleep improves, they are more relaxed and they manage to work through some of their worst memories of the war. At the time of our visit, Anna has worked with 345 soldiers, and almost all have said the same thing: that they recovered and relaxed after one session. 'Almost all who came back for a second session said their sleeping returned,' she says.

Commander Oleg is delighted with the results for his soldiers. 'When I was observing my boys today, I was thinking how their facial expressions were changing,' he says. 'I observed a positive effect, because they were turning from warriors to humans. A warrior needs to liquidate and a human needs to look at the world with harmony.'

It's not only soldiers who are suffering on the front lines. In many cases, the battles in Ukraine are being fought in cities and villages, not in trenches. These towns are full of families, schools and church groups, all of whom get caught up – and sometimes killed – as each side tries to destroy the other. For the people who live in a town that gets taken over or flattened, the war literally hits closer to home.

*

Someone who typifies the resilience of Ukrainians is Olya Kompanichenko. Sylvie and I first meet Olya at a community centre in Blistovitz, about an hour's drive from Kyiv and near Hostomel airport, where hundreds of Russian special forces soldiers arrived in helicopters in the first few hours of the invasion. For Ukrainians looking to the skies, it was an ominous moment.

Today when we meet Olya, she's working with others in the local council hall, making camouflage tents and screens. Scattered across the floor are boxes filled with hundreds of pieces of green and brown cloth. Olya and the group take the cloth out piece by piece and weave them together. The finished screens hang across the hall like clothes drying on a line in the sun. Ukrainian soldiers will use these to surround a small area in a forest where they have set up camp – obscuring any view of them should Russian soldiers be nearby. It's quite confronting to think that in a few days or weeks, these camouflage screens may make the difference between Ukrainian soldiers living or dying.

Community centres, council buildings and school halls across Ukraine have become crucial to the country's civilian army. In another hall we visited in Bucha we found locals making camouflage suits, the outfits that soldiers wear to blend in with bushes and greenery. As we walk around this hall with Olya, we see others making 'trench candles' with paraffin wax that soldiers can light to keep warm and cook with. They're small enough to be discreet so that Russian soldiers can't spot them and designed to burn slowly to last several hours.

This whole centre has become a war-response facility. In one room we see a playroom filled with toys. Many of the children around here are traumatised by the war, and locals have stocked this room with toys to give relief, a place where children can be children and not young people in a warzone. Another has been converted into a storage room and is brimming with donated goods: tinned food, bandages, teabags, blankets and row after row of chocolate. The locals insist we try it – it's tough to bite; dark but delicious. Those in the centre tell us the chocolate is important: soldiers spending months at the front line, often in freezing conditions, eating tinned food and stale bread night after night, need something to look forward to. A small indulgence in the middle of a big war.

After Olya shows us around the hall, she invites us to drive with her and Viktor, her husband, to their home, or at least what was their home. On that fateful day, 24 February, she and Viktor woke to the sound of explosions. Her brother's children were staying with them at the time. 'My brother called me and we realised that the war had started,' Olya says. 'We packed, put all the kids in the car and headed off.'

It was just as well they did. Two days later, their house suffered its first direct hit. Then came more, seven in total they discovered later from the shells around their house. The fact there had been seven direct hits suggests the Russians were deliberately targeting houses. It burnt down.

As we get out of the car to look around, Olya and Viktor fall silent. It's sad watching this couple as they walk slowly through the charred ruins of their home. Rooms where once their children slept. Sheds where once they kept gardening equipment. Stone walls dividing different parts of the garden now black from fire. Destroyed rooms and broken dreams.

It's not the first time Olya and Viktor have returned to look at the house. After several weeks of fighting, the Ukrainians forced the Russians from this area and the families were able to return. The deep sadness the couple feels is palpable. 'We had been very happy here. It was really hard the first time we came to see it after it was destroyed,' Olya says. 'I first came back without kids. It was really hard because my husband and I have been together for sixteen years, and for thirteen of those years we've been working on this house.'

Before the home and others around it had been destroyed, people in the area had formed a Facebook group to share information to help each other. But even after their neighbourhood was hit by missiles, they rallied together to help the soldiers who had moved on to different battlefronts. 'After we returned to this area – once the Russians were forced out – we used the Facebook group to gather things for the military, make camouflage nets, gather food supplies and medicine,' she says. 'We regularly load our cars and go to the hottest areas on the front line to bring all these supplies to the soldiers. The core of the neighbourhood group is about ten people, and others join in and participate. This is not a formally organised thing, it's just a group of people who wanted to help.'

I ask Olya how she holds their family together when something as integral as their home is destroyed. She says the first time she realised their house had been ruined was when a neighbour sent them a picture on WhatsApp. Olya's kids are 'quite mature' – her son is fifteen and her daughter is ten – so they didn't hide the news from them. 'My son received the news pretty calmly,' she says, 'but my daughter was upset and crying. When we came as a family to visit, my daughter looked around and went straight back to the car and said, "Get me out of here!" It was so hard, because this had been such a happy place.'

After intense fighting on the streets and in the skies, the Ukrainian forces eventually forced the Russian soldiers out of the towns surrounding Hostomel airport, leaving devastated neighbourhoods like Olya's behind. The war has now moved on to other fronts, but it's not just Ukrainians who are trying to save villages like Olya's. Soldiers from around the world are joining arms – and taking up arms – in the fight against Putin.

*

I'm on the outskirts of Kyiv with a group of fighters stalking the boundary of a building. They tell me that one of their colleagues inside has been shot and injured by Russian snipers, and they're trying to rescue him. They're well trained, fearsome-looking, and a key part of Ukraine's war effort, but they're not from Ukraine. These combatants are from Georgia and make up some of the thousands of soldiers who've come from around the world to Ukraine to fight the Russian army.

Without warning, the signal is given and the soldiers storm the building, with me running behind them. We encounter a firestorm of shooting and chaos. The group of soldiers runs into the building from different directions, with explosions and shouts of command ringing out through this otherwise quiet neighbourhood.

But luckily for all of us, there is no enemy behind these closed doors. This is a training exercise, although anyone walking by would not have known that from the ferocity of the action. The exercise is to practise extracting an injured soldier from enemy territory. While some of the fighters charge into the building, others wait outside, checking rooftops in case of snipers. Finally, after being covered by others in the team, four of the soldiers run out with the rescued soldier on a stretcher, rushing him into the back of an evacuation vehicle.

These sorts of training exercises are carried out in Ukraine and Russia every day, but what makes this particularly interesting is the foreign fighters taking part. These men and women are part of the 2000-strong Georgian National Legion who've come to Ukraine to join the fight against their old enemy, Russia. Of the thousands of volunteers backing up the Ukrainian army, the Georgian National Legion and the International Legion are making a particularly dramatic and direct contribution as they spend months in the mud, snow and misery of the front line. It's easy to tell upon meeting them that these are hard men and women.

The commander of the team is Sergeant Parmen Shulaia, a Georgian citizen. I ask him why so many fighters come from a country like Georgia and want to fight in someone else's war. He says that because Russia invaded his own country not so long ago, many Georgians are able to identify with the struggle of Ukrainians and their desire to repel Russia. 'Because of the aggression Georgians had at home, we know what Russians can do,' he says. 'In Georgia, every third or fourth family has someone who fought in the war against Russia starting from the 1990s.'

The Georgian National Legion has set up a base here on the outskirts of Kyiv. It's an old sprawling factory with several sheds and outhouses that have been turned into accommodation. Making my way through one shed, I walk past a room that has been turned into a makeshift bedroom. One fighter rests on a bed. Another uses a small gas bottle and a pan to fry eggs.

As I'm spending the day with these Georgian fighters, news comes through that a Ukrainian drone has hit the Kremlin. 'I want more!' Sergeant Shulaia says when I ask him for a reaction. As commander, Sergeant Shulaia says he tries to make sure that each team is a mixture of experienced fighters and novices. He says he carefully studies each volunteer to make sure they have the psychological strength and maturity to survive the front line. This, he says, is in everyone's interests – if it's a matter of life and death, no-one wants a colleague alongside them who can't be relied on when it really counts. 'All of the guys on this base who are training younger guys have already fought here in Ukraine, and some new ones are from Georgia,' he explains. 'We train them here with those experienced ones who have combat experience so they go together to fight.'

How does a group like this integrate with a formal army? 'With the Ukrainian army, we co-operate very well,' he says. 'We are fighting together, we don't have any problems … We are very tight. We have friends here; Ukrainians are our brothers. They're warriors, we fight with them.' I ask whether his fighters are happy. He tells me that they are. 'I will never say that someone's death makes me happy,' he says, 'but this war is completely different. I want our military victory.'

Sergeant Shulaia says the sort of training going on today is particularly valuable for volunteers who have little or no military experience. He himself made a difficult decision to leave home to come here to Ukraine to fight. 'I left a family in Georgia,' he explains. 'Three brothers – I'm the youngest – mother, father, all relatives in Georgia. But they're used to the fact that I'm not there.' He has left home on previous occasions to fight the Russians.

While these Georgian fighters have left their families 1500 kilometres away to fight an old foe, next I meet a couple who have travelled ten times that distance to support the Ukrainian war effort – they have come 15,000 kilometres, all the way from Tasmania.

I meet Rachel Lehmann Ware and her husband, Duncan Ware, in their high-rise apartment in an outer suburb of Kyiv. They're preparing another run of food and supplies to people in the north of the country. Months earlier they'd been teaching for a year at an international school in Kyiv when Russia invaded and, with their cats, had to make a dramatic three-week escape.

But back in Tasmania, their thoughts kept returning to the students and teachers with whom they had developed friendships.

Fragments of war

Top: Anti-corruption campaigner Viktor Barkholenko next to his bullet-damaged fence, and some of the tank shells that he has turned into flowerpots. He takes delight in turning something that once tried to kill his friends into things of beauty. *Bottom:* Hairdresser Vita Skynkariuk with the bullet casings she keeps as a daily reminder of the reality of the war.

Civilians doing their part

Clockwise from top left: Ashot Arushanov, a bikie who uses his motorbike to deliver supplies of water and food to the front lines. Max Stukalo, former marketing manager, who joined the Ukrainian army the day after Russia's invasion. His roles included counting dead Russian soldiers. Olya Kompanichenko, one of many civilians who are making camouflage gear in council halls across the country. And an unnamed volunteer testing a camouflage outfit.

Anton Chernysh (*top*) and one of Ukraine's first punk rockers, Oleksandr Pipa (*middle*), have swapped their music performances for making drones in a basement. Overnight they make spying, medical and attack drones while by day they test them. *Bottom:* Oleksandr showing author John Lyons a remote control for drones while testing his latest creations.

Life goes on

Top: We ran into soldier Kyril Slepzov after he joined an impromptu break-dancing party near Khreshchatyk metro station, Kyiv, while on his way home from the front lines. *Bottom:* Krystyna Orlova offered to help translate as Kyril told us of his love of dance. Krystyna, her husband and daughter had lived in Mariupol until it was destroyed in the three-month siege. She told us, 'We are very proud of our armed forces of Ukraine. All the time we're praying that they return alive and healthy.'

Friends Anastasiia Lebedenko (*left*) and Olena (*right*) fundraise for the war effort and, like many young Ukrainians, have stopped speaking Russian. The irony is that Putin's attempt to spread Russian culture has backfired among the war-affected younger Ukrainians, who are feeling greater Ukrainian national sentiment now than ever before.

Chef and former *MasterChef Ukraine* competitor Dmitri Shashenok (*left*) runs a steak restaurant in the Kyiv Food Market and says he would like nothing more than to fight Putin. Nataliia Stukalo (*right*) is one of Ukraine's most senior university executives. Within days of Russia's invasion, she worked with the country's academics to try to move classes online, to enable students to continue their courses as safely as possible and some academics who joined the army to continue their lectures from the front lines.

In an urban war like this, citizens go about their lives as best as possible, while mere kilometres away fierce fighting takes place. *Top:* Author John Lyons takes a break after interviewing Ukrainian soldiers whose job it is to shoot down incoming Russian drones and missiles. *Bottom:* Fighters from the Georgian National Legion, who have come to Ukraine from Georgia to join Ukraine's fight against Russia, train in the outskirts of Kyiv before going to the front line.

Contributing in every way they can

Top left: Maks Filatov was in the Ukrainian army until a shell destroyed his leg and he had to go home. He spends his days sitting with other wounded soldiers, listening, talking, being present. *Top right:* Artem Skorohodko runs the Behind Blue Eyes program, giving disposable cameras to war-affected children, asking them to document their war to help them talk about their experiences. *Bottom:* Ten-year-old Masha is part of the program. Her ten hamsters starved to death after Russian soldiers forced her family to flee, and now she holds backyard sales to pay for food for her new hamsters. *(Courtesy Behind Blue Eyes)*

Memories of the fallen

Top: Hundreds of Ukrainian flags, with the names of dead soldiers, in Independence Square in Kyiv. Families write the names of the soldiers and sometimes tributes.
Bottom: The Wall of Sorrow, near the famous golden-domed St Michael's monastery in the centre of Kyiv, which is covered with photographs of soldiers killed in battle.

Ukraine had a powerful pull on them, and when I meet them in their Kyiv home, they're delighted to be back. 'We were always determined to come back,' Rachel says. 'It was just a matter of when, and when it was safe.' As she makes coffee in the kitchen, she seems completely comfortable in this city. 'Coming back to Ukraine, it just feels like we've come home.'

Upon their return to Kyiv, Rachel immediately noticed the effects of war. She and Duncan returned to their old school but could tell that many of their students had suffered the stress of war either directly or through others. Many schools across the country tried to carry on as normally as possible. 'There has been some very clear impact on my students from this war, emotionally and also academically,' she says. She recalls one of her year six students being scared because his father worked as an engineer at one of the energy plants in Dnipro, where Russian forces launched attacks on critical infrastructure. 'There were bombing attacks happening during school time,' she says. 'And he just didn't know if his dad was alive and was clearly upset and quite traumatised.'

Some children at the school were diagnosed with PTSD. 'There's been a lot of mental health issues for these children,' she says. 'We have thankfully, though, got a wonderful psychologist at our school who helps them and is there for them. But I must say, the resilience of these kids is mind-blowing.'

Many of Rachel's colleagues at the school have been directly touched by the war. One of the school's security guards joined the Ukrainian forces on the front line, and a staff member's sister was in Irpin when it was under attack. 'She went through absolute hell getting out of there. Their car was shot up. They barely got out with their lives.'

Beyond trying to give their students' studies some normalcy, Rachel and Duncan also joined a humanitarian group called Vans Without Borders. Through them they connected with Oleh, a Chernihiv local who is trying to help his town rebuild. Chernihiv was heavily damaged by Russian missiles, so Rachel and Duncan bought a van to help transport building supplies so they could create new homes. 'You've got mothers with kids sleeping on the floor in a friend's house or in the cellar because they just haven't got a house to go to,' she says.

Rachel says she was struck by the 'unbelievable strength' of Ukrainians. 'The attempt by Putin to eradicate Ukrainian culture has had the reverse effect,' she says. 'No-one speaks Russian anymore. Everyone is speaking Ukrainian. And it's just this real sense of pride in their culture. I think that's one of the reasons we love it here so much and why we wanted to return.'

Wherever you go in Ukraine you find people doing their bit for the war effort, whether they are citizens or not. There are volunteer chefs making food to be taken to the front line, cooking huge pots of soups, rice, casseroles and vegetables. Many Russians and Ukrainians who follow the war at the front line concede that Ukrainian soldiers eat better than Russian soldiers. 'One thing I can tell you is that the Ukrainian soldiers eat well,' says Cyrile Amoursky, a French-Russian journalist who's spent time at the Ukrainian front line. In a documentary he made, Ukrainian soldiers tell how much a well-cooked meal served hot lifts their spirits.

From stockpiles of chocolate being sent to the front line to hot meals being served by volunteer chefs, the Ukraine people's army is being supported in every way its citizens know how. But not everyone has the ability or resources to drop everything they're doing to join the war effort. Around the country, there are hundreds of thousands of people who must stay employed to keep the nation running despite Russia's invasion. People still need to buy groceries. People still need to pay their bills. People still need to access healthcare. So while some are sewing flak jackets or digging trenches, for others the best resistance is waking up every day and simply going to work.

If there's one thing every Ukrainian we meet wants to do it's live their everyday lives as normally as possible.

CHAPTER 3

Life in wartime

FINDING THEMSELVES AT THE CENTRE OF THE FIRST LAND war in Europe since World War II, Ukrainians have been determined to keep one thing alive: joy. It's been a conscious decision. This has been no easy task, yet Ukrainians see it as vital to victory. They are reminded daily of the horrors of war: injured soldiers with prosthetic legs hobble around large cities, people push family members in wheelchairs, and air-raid sirens force people to pull their children from their beds throughout the night. But one thing Sylvie and I found uplifting in our time here in Ukraine is the joy.

Soon upon arriving in Ukraine, you notice the search for opportunities to celebrate life. For us, nobody better personifies this joie de vivre than the young soldier we've come across on this Friday night near one of Kyiv's biggest train stations.

It's a warm spring evening in Kyiv and a crowd has gathered at the Khreshchatyk metro station, a popular gathering place for young people. On this night, about a hundred people are standing in a circle watching an impromptu break-dancing performance. While the crowd sings and dances with the performers, on the sideline we notice a soldier stands watching. Then, without warning, he puts down his bulging army kitbag, runs into the centre and begins to break-dance. It's stunning. The crowd erupts in the kind of spontaneous outbreak of delight that we kept seeing across Ukraine. All eyes are on him as people clap and cheer him on.

When he takes a break, we see a woman walk through the crowd and give him some water. She tries to put some cash into his pocket but he refuses to take it. What the woman is trying to do reflects something we also see over and over: people wanting to support soldiers in whatever way they can. Ukrainians feel a deep of affection, respect and gratitude for their soldiers.

We approach the soldier to speak to him. His name is Kyril Slepzov, a 27-year-old who's just returned from the front line for a three-week break. He hasn't even been home yet. He was on his way to the train station when he came across this outdoor party and decided to join in.

'Dancing was one of my hobbies at school,' Kyril tells us, 'and now my hobby is protecting Ukraine. After four months at the front line, I now have the opportunity of being here and am on my way to Dnipro, my home city. In Ukraine at the moment, we try to live our lives no matter what happens.'

*

Shelves of Ukraine's finest wines line the walls as families wander through the food hall, choosing between stalls selling cooked steaks, Vietnamese pho, cupcakes and coffee. Walking around this magnificent market in the late afternoon sun, one can briefly forget that this is a country at war.

On sunny weekends, thousands of people walk the parks and malls of Kyiv, often with babies in prams. Extended families are highly valued here in Ukraine, with several generations sometimes living together and going on joint outings.

Nowhere highlights this as starkly as the magnificent Kyiv Food Market. This large renovated warehouse showcases twenty different food outlets and bars. During the day, its magnificent wine and food stalls are packed with families, which typifies Kyiv's double life under war: the people who are here eating steak with red wine at midday may be the same people in bunkers somewhere at 3 am. Ukrainians tell me they hope Putin sees pictures of them carrying on their lives normally, not cowering in bomb shelters. They say they are convinced nothing will upset the Russian leader more than realising that they are continuing with their lives largely as normal.

Visitors to Kyiv are often surprised that this is a city at war. Former Australian army officer Robert Potter says on first appearances, everything can seem normal. 'We have this image in our head of conflict being in remote and regional places, happening in deserts, happening in jungles,' Potter tells me. 'But this is an urban war with the vast majority of fighting happening in an urban environment. We're seeing what is essentially a beautiful European capital turned into a warzone, and buildings that were built by the Soviet Union or Ukrainian architects being turned into fortified positions.'

Potter has spent considerable time in Kyiv helping Ukrainians to protect their cyber systems. David Robinson, Potter's co-founder of the Australian cyber security company Internet 2.0, who has also spent months here, contrasts Ukraine with areas in which he served in the Australian army. 'Every war has a population that still needs to make money and needs to function,' Robinson explains. 'Everyone imagines war to be like the movies – constant – but those are only small pockets of areas in large countries at war.' He remembers that when he was in Iraq in the Australian army, Baghdad still functioned as a normal city – it was more violent and dangerous than Kyiv but the economy needed to keep ticking along. Ukraine is similar. 'I think their courage and resolve is why they get to do what they do now,' he says, 'which is to live relatively normal lives in their cities despite the bombing.'

In Kyiv, you quickly learn the reality of air-raid sirens and the rush to bunkers; it becomes second nature. My first experience of the war was something I won't forget. I was staying at the 11 Mirrors Design Hotel, owned by the colourful mayor of Kyiv, Vitali Klitschko, a one-time world heavyweight boxing champion. I was on the top floor having breakfast with David Robinson when we heard explosions. 'That's incoming,' says David, having had much experience of incoming fire in Iraq. We wait a few seconds and hear more. It's loud and in the Kyiv area.

'Is that close?' I ask Robinson.

'Not really,' he replies. 'Probably five to ten kilometres.'

The three Ukrainian men at the next table quickly leave. We're the only people left in the restaurant. 'We should go,' Robinson says. 'We'll use the stairs and grab anything we need from our rooms as we go down.'

I have with me my constant companion when I'm on assignment, my mobile journalism video equipment, or mojo for short. It's essentially a mobile phone rigged up with sound equipment and an app called LiveU, which allows me to connect to the ABC so that I can go live on the News Channel within seconds. Sometimes from Ukraine I've been able to go live with a breaking story within ten minutes of a major development. This technology will never replace the work of camera operators and serious TV studios, but it's part of the future – it means a reporter can break and then analyse major news in real time. For me it's been a liberation in an era when people want instant news and instant analysis.

So I reach into my backpack and turn on my mojo. I walk behind Robinson as we make our way down the stairs, collecting things from our rooms as we go. Robinson wants to grab a laptop; I want my flak jacket. It may sound a strange thing to think of in the circumstances – a flak jacket won't do much if a missile rips through the hotel – but one of the most difficult things for a media organisation in a warzone is getting insurance for its staff. It can cost US$500 a day, and one of the conditions of the ABC's insurance is that we must wear our flak jackets if confronted with imminent danger – and an air-raid siren constitutes imminent danger. One photo of me in a bunker without my flak jacket could void our insurance, so on it goes.

Old-timer correspondents scoff at this, saying the last thing that you should think about in a warzone is your organisation's insurance. My response is that in a warzone you need to think of many things, and your own organisation's ability to keep sending correspondents to a place like this should be one of them. There may, of course, be times when you need to run straight to a bunker and don't have time to get a flak jacket, but on this occasion, we're running by my room, so there's really no excuse.

Enduring missile attacks in the 11 Mirrors Design Hotel was different from experiencing them in other parts of the country. While some bunkers were simply concrete-reinforced pits in the ground or carparks underneath apartment buildings, many of Kyiv's bunkers were designed with the view that they should make life as pleasant as possible for the new and likely long-term wartime reality.

The 11 Mirrors' bomb shelter had an amenity one would not usually expect during a war: room service. Staff made clear to those in the bunker that this was all part of making life as normal as possible. On one occasion, a guest who had rushed to the bunker had ordered lunch before the incoming-missile alert. When the siren sounded, he headed straight for the basement. He was stunned – and very pleased – when staff appeared in the bunker with his lunch order: a steak tartare with a glass of pinot noir. For some no service is spared during times of war.

*

It is in the most extraordinary cheese shop in Kyiv that Sylvie and I meet someone who gives me brilliant insights into her country's war effort. It is the presentation of the shop that draws us in, huge wheels of cheese hanging in the windows as part of a magnificent display.

It is about sixteen months since Putin invaded and we've just arrived back in Kyiv on a train from Poland, so the sensitivities are new once again. As we walk through the city we notice this remarkable shop. There are scores of cheese wheels displayed by region, from France to Italy, Poland and Ukraine. There are soft cheeses, hard cheeses and even green cheeses, which the shop assistant explains are young. Inside, the air is cool and keeping all the milk products at the perfect temperature.

On entering the shop we meet Nataliia Stukalo, a customer who's shopping for a dinner she's hosting that evening. The scene typifies the sentiment of so many Ukrainians. Dinners, birthdays and anniversaries are to be celebrated. The assistant in the shop is going around the store curating an extraordinary smorgasbord of fine cheeses for Nataliia.

Nataliia welcomes us to Kyiv and, like so many other Ukrainians, is delighted to have foreigners in the country. Wherever we travel we find that Ukrainians want as many people from overseas as possible to come. It is almost like a form of insurance, a protection of sorts: the more of us that are in the country, the more chance there is of the world knowing about this war. A visceral fear of many Ukrainians – including President Volodymyr Zelensky – is that the world may become fatigued by the war and begin to forget about it. And if the world forgets about the war, it will stop funding and supporting Ukraine.

Beneath the surface, Nataliia and millions of other Ukrainians are working systematically to support the war effort. In her case, it turns out she is playing a particularly unique role – one of Ukraine's leading academics in charge of the university sector. As the deputy head of the National Agency for Higher Education Quality Assurance, an agency that implements the Ukrainian government's higher education policy, the war threw her life and the institutions that she advises into chaos. Her insights are key to us understanding how both academics and students have responded to the war effort.

Until the war, Nataliia's life was crowded with the sorts of meetings you'd expect from one of Ukraine's most senior university figures. She lives in the centre of Kyiv and enjoys the best of this city. In early 2022, she'd heard suggestions in the media that Russia was preparing an invasion, but like most Ukrainians, the notion of Vladimir Putin ordering a full-scale attack seemed close to impossible. 'Nobody here believed that it would start,' she says. 'We really did not see the reason why, so what is the reason? We are a peaceful nation, we have chosen our way to work and live, so what would be the reason for an invasion?'

The Kremlin had often engaged in sabre-rattling, and Moscow had invaded Crimea in 2014 – successfully, from Moscow's point of view. The international community had done nothing to repel the Russian invasion of Crimea. From Putin's point of view, he'd faced no resistance. But a full-scale invasion of Ukraine, across its eastern border? Many Ukrainians thought this would be an act of madness that even Putin, for all his talk about re-establishing the glory of the old Soviet empire, would see as a bridge too far.

But that bridge was not too far after all, and when the invasion began, ordinary Ukrainians rallied to fight. The reason this volunteer army emerged overnight is encapsulated in a phrase that we hear from Ukrainians over and over: if Russians put down their guns, the war would be over, but if Ukrainians put down their guns, they would no longer have a country. Russia would take over their country, as they almost did in those first days of the war. What is fascinating about Ukraine's defence of itself is that two separate armies emerged overnight: the army at the front line and the massive behind-the-scenes programs that helped to keep the Ukrainian army and economy strong. The home front, literally.

On 24 February 2022, Nataliia was woken around 4.30 am by the sound of text messages on her phone: 'The war has started,' one university colleague said. One of Nataliia's first thoughts was that the city centre would be one of Russia's major targets. She lives near the presidential palace, surely a target for Russian missiles. She turned on the news to see that indeed Kyiv was under attack, as well as Dnipro in Ukraine's east. Her parents and brothers lived in Dnipro, so Nataliia made an instant decision: she would meet her son, who was also in Kyiv as a student, and they would make the five-hour drive to Dnipro where she could be near her family and look after her elderly parents.

Once she had made these personal decisions, she made a major professional one: Ukraine's universities would immediately go to an online-learning model so lecturers and students could continue their education from the safest place they could find. Covid had set a template for how to study remotely, so those students and lecturers who did not head to army recruitment offices found places removed from immediate danger to try to continue their courses. For many this meant leaving Kyiv and eastern parts of the country and heading to remote rural areas or a city such as Lviv in the far west, less in the firing line than cities like Kyiv, Dnipro, Kherson and Kharkiv.

The university sector had been thrown into chaos. The war dislodged not just many of the country's students but academics too. 'I know a lot of professors, even rectors and even my colleagues from the national agency who went to the front,' Nataliia said. 'I know one professor who went to the front on the very first day of the full-scale invasion, and he even gave lectures from the trenches.' To try to ensure that his students' university courses were not disrupted because he had gone to join the war, that professor continued to lecture from the front line. Nataliia told us that he would try to find a safe spot sufficiently away from the trenches so as not to endanger other soldiers; tracking wi-fi and phone signals was one way that both Russian and Ukrainian armies tried to discover where their enemies were hiding. The professor would use his phone to connect to his students and worked through the curriculum over several months. For him, this was a victory over the Kremlin.

During the battle of Bakhmut, Nataliia received a phone call from a friend who was still in the eastern city. They told her that they were in the building of one of the universities and noticed there was a very good library and some expensive computers. Worrying that the building would be destroyed or looted, they asked to speak with someone at the university to co-ordinate moving the books and equipment to a safer place.

'I put him in contact with the rector of that university and those soldiers helped to save the libraries and those books,' she says. 'They put them in their cars and sent them to safer places so the university could pick them up at some point. Our army wanted to save the books. We want our people to read books, to study and to have an educated future and a future among European countries.'

This shows the importance Ukraine places on education, even during wartime. In fact, much of the foreign campaign to maintain support for Ukraine has been driven by the country's universities. One of the most powerful projects on the international stage is *Unissued Diplomas*, an exhibition featuring scores of young

Ukrainian students who were completing their university degrees but then died in the war before they could collect their diplomas. The exhibition travels the world and helps to raise money for the Ukrainian army. It was organised by undergraduates still living in Ukraine and relies on Ukrainian students studying around the world organising exhibitions with their host universities.

Yana Mokhonchuk, an intern at the Ukrainian embassy in Canberra, helped bring the exhibition to Australia. As we wander through it at the University of Sydney, Yana says those behind the project wanted to remind us of the efforts of so many Ukrainian students on the front lines. The primary objective was to commemorate those who sacrificed for their country.

The loss of life the project documents gives a powerful insight into the destruction this war has wrought on the younger generation of Ukrainians. It has devastated much of the next generation of adults. Story after story tells of senseless lost youth and potential. These were young, smart and dedicated people who had chosen fields of study on which they wanted to base their adult lives, but they had it all cut down by Putin's greed.

This exhibition reminds me of the first time I walked alongside the gravestones of fallen Australian soldiers at Gallipoli. Among the carefully manicured lawns, I was struck by the youth of so many of the dead – seventeen, eighteen, one even fourteen. Many young Australians had lied about their age in order to go to Europe to fight. Likewise, we discovered in Ukraine that many young people were desperate to join the front line to defend their country. Some who had medical conditions that might preclude them from joining even tried to bribe recruiters to allow them to serve.

Many of those remembered in the *Unissued Diplomas* exhibition enlisted to join the army and died in combat shortly after joining the war. But many were also civilian deaths, killed by Russian missiles that hit their homes or cars. As I walk around the exhibition in Sydney, I find the details of those killed to be confronting. Each one is a story worth acknowledging, but they make for heavy reading:

Ivanna Obodzinska, nineteen, studied landscape architecture, and died alongside her twin babies when two Russian missiles hit her house.

Hliv Ivanov, twenty-one, studied political science, joined the armed forces of Ukraine with his father on the second day of the war. He died in the battle of Bakhmut.

Vladyslav Lisniak, twenty-six, studied accounting and taxation. His ambition was to join the army and become an officer. When the invasion occurred, he enlisted and died while providing cover for his unit, which had to withdraw from Mariupol because of Russia's overwhelming firepower. He was posthumously awarded the Order of Courage by President Zelensky.

Serhiy Domantsevych, twenty, studied agronomy. His dream was 'graduating, finding love and getting a job in the IT sector'. For fun he ran a YouTube channel about video games. After the Russians attacked Chernihiv, Serhiy and others spent two weeks in a shelter trying to avoid incoming missiles. Finally, the group decided to leave the shelter and run for safety. As they did, they were killed by a Russian missile.

Taras Stakhiv, eighteen, studied English philology and wanted to become a translator. He rushed to the front within the first weeks and died in the Donetsk region three days before his nineteenth birthday.

Ivan Pokidko, nineteen, was studying at the Ukrainian Leadership Academy. He'd written in his diary, 'I will create the world around me by myself.' He died from a Russian airstrike and was awarded the Order of Courage by President Zelensky.

Lidiia Duminika, seventeen, studied food science. She planned to open a pastry shop where she would bake cakes using her own recipes. She died in Mykolaiv from a Russian multiple rocket launcher.

Daniil Shmahlii, seventeen, studied medicine. His ambition was to be 'an outstanding surgeon'. He died after jumping off the Irpin Bridge to escape Russian shelling.

Valentyn Yakymchuk, eighteen, studied tourism. He was about to begin driving lessons. Russian soldiers shot him with an armoured-vehicle gun.

Emir Bilyalov, seventeen, studied computer technology. His hobby was producing both traditional and digital art. He died in the first few hours of the invasion, when a Russian shell hit his family's home in Kherson.

Maksym Vasyleshyn, eighteen, studied international relations. He aimed to create a 'business empire' related to construction, machinery and cars. In the early days of the war he joined the Azov regiment to help to defend Kyiv. He was killed in Kharkiv.

Danyyil Yevtushenko, nineteen, studied philosophy. He learnt foreign languages, played several musical instruments and sang. In the first days of the invasion he enlisted in the Territorial Defence Forces, despite having no military experience. He told friends, 'When somebody asks me where I was during the war, I will not be ashamed – I defended Ukraine.' He died under Russian rocket attack in Kharkiv.

Kyrylo Osipenko, twenty-two, studied computer science. In 2014, Kyrylo and his mother fled their home in Donetsk to safety in Kharkiv after Russian forces invaded. A week after the 2022 invasion, Kyrylo was killed in a Russian missile attack in Kharkiv.

Oleksandr Kotsukon, twenty-two, studied journalism. He was planning a holiday with his mother and they were about to get matching tattoos. He loved driving, so when the invasion occurred he enlisted as a driver for a patrol battalion. He died defending Mariupol.

Dymytro Yevdokymov, twenty-three, studied US and European studies. He enlisted immediately upon the invasion. 'I cannot betray what I believe in and what I love,' he said at the time. He died in one of the battles of Kharkiv. He was awarded the Order of Courage by President Zelensky.

Oleksandra Borivska, eighteen, studied international relations. She wanted a career in the diplomatic service and her friends said she liked to take care of stray animals, often taking food to them. She was killed by a Russian missile attack on Vinnytsia while on her way to a driving lesson.

Andriy Dalibozhko, twenty-three, studied agronomy. Andriy, his father, brother and a friend died when Russian soldiers shot at their car near Chornobaivka.

Mykyta Perebyinis, eighteen, studied software engineering. He was killed by mortar fire near Kyiv.

Iryna Dashko, twenty, studied agronomy. A brilliant cook, she was planning to marry her boyfriend in the spring. She was killed by a Russian bomb near Kyiv.

Tetiana Kotlubei, twenty, studied computer science. Her ambition was to study overseas and get a master's degree. She died in Mariupol when a Russian artillery shell hit the house she was in.

Viktor Shapovalov, twenty, studied accounting and taxation. After the invasion, he enlisted in the army to help fight the Russian army from Mariupol. He died when a Russian bomb hit his trench during a combat mission. He was awarded the Order of Courage by President Zelensky.

Yevheniia Babakova, twenty, studied pharmacy. Her ambition was to open a pharmacy and massage centre. Her hobbies were making TikTok videos and bead embroidery. She was killed by a Russian airstrike on Mariupol.

Polina Zheldak, twenty, studied English. Her ambitions included opening a study centre and spending time by the sea with her boyfriend, Yevhen. She died under rubble after Russian missiles hit residential buildings in Chernihiv.

Danylo Prokopenko, nineteen, studied information technology. He worked in IT and his hobby was cycling. He died in Izyum after receiving a head wound from a Russian artillery shell.

Matvi Levchuk, twenty-five, studied management. His hobbies were growing indoor plants and fishing. His aim was to be a professional soldier. After the invasion he enlisted and served as a master sergeant in a border detachment. He died in a trench in Donetsk when hit by a Russian projectile.

The word that keeps going through my head as I read all these life tributes is 'senseless'. Putin's march of destruction cut a swathe through the best and brightest in Ukraine. These young people represented hope for their future and their country. So much energy, so much drive, so many dreams, so much potential – all cut down by the scythe of war. Putin is the grim reaper in absentia in this room.

For me the saddest story of all is that of twenty-year-old Leah Krylova. The biographies that accompany all the other memorials in this exhibition are based on interviews with surviving family and friends. Leah's panel is different. Apart from the degree she was studying, she had no backstory, nothing about her interests or ambitions. Leah had been studying tourism at Mariupol State University. A Russian shell hit her father's house in Mariupol, killing Leah, her sister, her father, her boyfriend and several of her friends. As the panel under her photo notes, 'We don't know Leah's story because she died with her whole family and now there is no-one to tell her story.'

Ukrainians are living with a growing bank of memorials. They live with these memories even as they try to get on with their daily lives.

*

Tucked among cafés and apartment buildings in a quiet part of Kyiv is a barber shop popular with the city's trendy crowd. After several weeks in Ukraine, I need a haircut, and a British journalist has recommended this place. And so one afternoon I walk up the stairs to discover one of the funkiest barber shops I've ever been to.

Sylvie and I are greeted by Vita Skynkariuk, a Ukrainian woman in her late twenties who offers us a coffee. Surrounding the shampoos and conditioners around her desk we notice an extraordinary display: a collection of used bullets. She's put them together as a daily reminder of the war going on a few hours' drive away.

Before the Russian invasion, Vita, like many Ukrainians, had been aware of the danger of an increasingly aggressive Russia. But she had lived with that ominous feeling for the last eight years since the invasion of Crimea and parts of eastern Ukraine, so the real dread of a Russian invasion didn't hit home until it happened. 'Until the morning of the twenty-fourth,' she says, 'I could not believe it.'

Vita says that at first glance, someone walking around Kyiv would have the impression that Ukrainians are getting on with their lives. 'You can meet in the restaurants or even in the bars, but behind the scenes I do not know anyone who does not do something for the war.' Everybody donates or makes posts on Instagram; when they hear the news that someone they know is at the front line, they spread the news on social media. 'We send money, or on our birthdays, instead of receiving a present from friends, we ask to make a parcel for the needs for particular brigades,' she says. 'This is the way regular people can help our army.'

Daily life has changed in some ways but not others. 'At night we can hear explosions,' she says. 'We go to work and we go out sometimes, but the war is the first thing that we think about each day.' I find Vita's attitude positive and determined: she supports the war effort in every way she can, but she also sees the importance of going about her daily life as if her country were not at war. To let the Russians take away her joy would be letting Putin win. 'Our choice is either we die or we move on with our lives,' she says. 'But I can say that there is no-one in Ukraine who is untouched by this war. In our private conversations the war is the most important thing we think about, and not just talking but helping.'

We ask Vita, as a hairdresser in Kyiv, what she would say to a fellow hairdresser in Moscow if she had the chance. 'I would like to calmly touch the heart of the Russian people,' she says. But at the same time, Vita says she hopes one day Russians will realise that President Putin is 'an insane person, extremely violent'.

Vita grew up in a patriotic family that used more Ukrainian language than Russian. But most of her friends used to speak

Russian, so she did the same. That changed when the war began: most Ukrainians I spoke to have switched to Ukrainian, and they're prouder than ever of their country. 'Today I can say a hundred per cent I am deeply committed to my people, my land, my language, everything I have here,' she says. 'I do not want to live anywhere else. I want to live in this country, my country. I want to build something here, I want to create something here, I want people around me to feel the same, love the land and want to create something for that land. We live among good people, strong people, intelligent people, and we have everything to build a strong future here.'

Vita's boyfriend, Anton Semenenko, also sees resilience and resistance to Russia's invasion and occupation as 'normal'. Today he's dropped in at lunchtime for a coffee with Vita. 'We can think about bad things all the time – the bombs and the shellings are everyday situations,' he tells us. 'But I think it can be dangerous to dwell too much about things as they are now ... Each morning you get out of bed and try to live as normal a day as possible. This is our life now, and if possible, we need to stay positive.'

Ukrainian after Ukrainian told me that one of the best ways to keep hopeful is to keep busy. Two of Anton's friends volunteer by driving cars with supplies of food, clothing and medicines to the front line. Anton says that on top of volunteering and fundraising, most Ukrainians have made the decision to try to continue their regular lives as much as they can, particularly when it comes to their work and paying taxes. He says there is a widespread view that Ukrainians need to keep the economy as strong as a wartime economy can be; without a working economy and the taxes that come from it, the country would find it difficult to keep paying for its army. This is particularly important in case international support decreases over time, other wars break out and the world grows weary of funding the Ukrainian effort. Ukraine must try to set its war effort onto a sustainable foundation in case the war drags on for years. He welcomes the Ukraine government's move to put in place special exemption and payment plans for people finding it difficult to pay taxes. 'The government is trying to make it easier for common citizens, but I have not heard of anyone who has not paid it,' he says. 'Everyone is determined to try to keep paying all their taxes.'

Frequently during the war President Zelensky has specifically said to Ukrainians to do whatever they can to keep the economy strong, both to provide employment and to help to pay for the war effort.

Another of those who emphasises a strong economy is Max Stukalo, the marketing manager who quit his lucrative job to lead an army unit and ended up counting the bodies of dead Russian soldiers. I ask whether there's any resentment from soldiers at the front line seeing other Ukrainians enjoying what appears to be a good life in the cafés, restaurants and nightclubs of Kyiv.

'For me, as a soldier who saw a lot of death and destruction in our country, it was not easy,' he admits. 'Every second at the front line can be death, but at the same time, people are sitting in cafés two hundred kilometres away.'

Max had to return from the front line when he was badly injured in an explosion, including being temporarily blinded in both eyes. When he got out of hospital, he struggled to be in the streets with people living their normal lives while his army colleagues were doing it so tough at the front. 'But I know that the economy of Ukraine is part of the fighting too,' he says. 'If there is money, if there are jobs and everything is working, that is better for the country as it allows us to keep funding our army. The economy is a key part of our war effort.'

The apparent normality of daytime life in Ukraine has brought its own problems. On social media – where these days so much opinion is shaped, particularly of younger people – there was considerable criticism after photos were published of Ukrainians crowding into McDonald's stores and other eating places. What I had not known until I spent time there is that in Ukraine, McDonald's is seen as a corporate hero for closing its outlets in Russia soon after the invasion. Ukrainians delighted in the idea that Vladimir Putin might see them sitting around eating in a McDonald's.

In trying to keep the economy ticking, nightclubs and restaurants still open in the evening, but they close at 11 pm when a curfew kicks in. As many young people tell us, this is done out of respect for soldiers at the front line. They realise it would be bad for morale if soldiers saw pictures of people partying through the night while they fight.

In some ways, having a drink at a bar became its own form of rebellion. Robert Potter, the Australian cyber expert we met earlier, started a tradition of 'rocket night' at a local wine bar, which became famous in defence circles in Kyiv: if Russia fires missiles into Kyiv, then the following night everyone in this social group is encouraged to go to the bar as a show of defiance to Putin. These nights are at a bar opposite the hotel where I stayed, so I would sometimes join 'rocket night'.

There is a fascinating energy to these evenings, with both expatriates and locals partying hard and almost driven by an anger and determination that Putin will not win. It became clear to me that the stress of a country at war can feed into a determination that people are able to unwind with a drink, often also for soldiers to have a break from the front line. After a rapid-fire few hours of hard drinking, when 11 pm and the curfew comes around, people empty from most of the bars and go home. The same young men and women who preen themselves for a few hours of cocktails and banter may well find themselves in a bomb shelter two or three hours later.

This doesn't mean, of course, that some do not break the rules. As an expatriate in Kyiv, you hear of some nightclubs that party through the night, particularly as the war drags on. And true to human nature, some people try to make money even out of the most difficult of circumstances. I heard about clubs around Kyiv that stayed open despite the curfew and would call on soldiers to double as taxi drivers to take patrons home; if you're escorted home by someone in the army, you won't be fined for breaking the curfew. But your expense for a night out? A soldier-driven taxi ride home that might normally cost US$10 could be US$200 instead.

Is this corruption? The Ukrainian soldiers making money from the 5 am taxi rides argue that this money enables them to survive on an otherwise meagre army salary. Other Ukrainians argue that rules are rules: the 11 pm curfew is there for a reason. Even if soldiers were driving them home, it would erode the morale of the troops at the front knowing people were dancing and drinking at nightclubs around Ukraine until sunrise.

Those who do stick to the curfew spend their evenings in their homes. But unfortunately, that doesn't mean they are getting much sleep.

*

Nowhere is night and day more starkly defined than Ukraine. Most of Russia's missile and drone attacks happen at night, usually around 3 am. That's the toughest time for 22-year-old

Anastasiia Lebedenko, the translator we met earlier. Like many Ukrainians, she hasn't slept well since the war started. 'That's part of living in a country at war,' she says. 'You can't even rely on getting a good night's sleep.'

Sylvie and I meet Anastasiia and her friend Olena relaxing at a café in Kyiv. Neither of them is sleeping well. Anastasiia says that unlike some of her friends, she has not psychologically adapted to war. She has friends who don't flinch at air-raid sirens anymore, even when there are loud explosions. 'They have got used to the sirens and don't react at all, because their psyche would break if they reacted every time,' she says. 'They would not be able to keep going with their work and their life.' But Anastasiia just can't switch off her nervous system's fight-or-flight response. And even on the nights without sirens, she still lies awake, anxious that she might not hear the siren in time. Instead, she says, 'I might wake up to the sound of explosions.'

The night before we meet, Anastasiia has had a particularly bad night. There was an air-raid siren at 3 am. Most nights, after a siren goes off, she moves to the bathroom, but she cannot sleep properly in there. 'So [most nights] I stay there and check the news to see what's flying where,' she explains. But last night, when she heard the siren, she packed her things and went to a metro station deep underground. She slept there until 5.30 am, then went home and slept in her bed till 10 am, which is when she had to start work.

'The last two weeks have been exhausting with the nightly attacks, because I wake up really out of it and then I have to carry on with my day,' Anastasiia explains. 'You don't know what will happen at night, and for me, that is the most psychologically exhausting thing. That I have to keep working, to keep living, no matter the external circumstances.'

She thinks the Russians attacking between 3 and 4 am is a deliberate psychological tactic – it's when most people are in their deepest stage of sleep, and when you wake up from a deep sleep it is much harder to get back to sleep. 'You are just shattered, and the insomnia carries on to the next day,' Anastasiia says. 'They are stealing from all of us every day. They know all of us are shattered, and they consciously do so.'

Anastasiia's friend Olena has learnt to live with night-time explosions in Kyiv. 'My first instinct is to run away and hide and to make a conscious choice not to think about death,' she says. But that doesn't make her want to run away from Ukraine – she's determined to stay. 'It's possible that I may die, but for some reason I want to be in my homeland … As a kind of meditation, I like to concentrate more on the value of my positive emotions and faith. I sometimes don't know why I believe that everything will be okay, but I have faith that it will be.'

In the first week of war, one of Anastasiia's friends decided that she 'would not let Russians spoil my life'; Anastasiia tries to think the same way. 'They want us to regress, to give up, and every day when we choose not to it's an act of defiance,' she says. 'Going to work is an act of courage, because in these circumstances it's easy to give up.'

Like many Ukrainians in their twenties and thirties, Anastasiia is active in fundraising to buy soldiers at the front whatever they need: medical kits, food, water, generators, even vehicles. 'There's a saying that for Russia it's only soldiers fighting, but for Ukraine there's a whole nation fighting, because it's not simply our soldiers on the front line,' she says. 'It's also everyone supporting their men and women and supporting their effort to keep going.'

Olena uses her skills as a graphic designer and illustrator to take part in art initiatives, the proceeds of which are donated to the military. She was also part of an exhibition in Berlin that donated money to the army. 'It's trying to make little choices that can help,' she says. 'Our country is alive. A lot of people are here. We donate, we live our lives, and we are not looking like Russia scares us. No, we are not fucking scared: we are okay. We are confident that everything will be okay, and we are doing everything we can to support our country.'

If it wasn't for this citizen army and the people donating to it, Anastasiia's childhood home could have been destroyed. She describes how in her hometown, Mykolaiv, the city didn't end up in the hands of Russians because civilians organised effectively. 'They say the only reason Mykolaiv didn't fall is because the city was so supportive of the effort.' Now living in Kyiv, she wants to continue to bolster the efforts of the soldiers.

'I have my life here in Kyiv because these people are protecting me every day, giving their lives,' Anastasiia says. 'They're fighting for me to keep living my life, so I have to support them in what they're doing. It's a cause and effect: if I don't support them, the fight would not be going on. Every Ukrainian feels obliged to support in any way possible – physical, moral – for the fight to keep going.'

Defiance is one word that Anastasiia says defines modern Ukraine. She recalls the videos of people trying to stop tanks by standing in front of them. To her, it feels natural. 'If someone comes to your home and invades it, do you just give it up or do you fight?' she asks. 'Of course you will fight – it is not even a question.' She thinks that a lot of Ukrainians have discovered that they are stronger than they thought. 'The Russians want to erase us, to erase our identity, to merge us together. We don't want this. We want to stay ourselves, to live on our land, to live by our values and to build our path as we see it. We realise the value of what we have and who we are.'

Nearly everyone we spoke to shared this view – that since this war with Russia, they have felt 'more Ukrainian'. Traditionally, Russians and Ukrainians have been closely coupled because of their shared Soviet past; anyone over the age of forty would have spent at least some of their life living under Soviet rule, speaking the Russian language, eating Russian food and listening to Russian music. For many decades, Russian was seen as a more intellectual and sophisticated language – the language of Tolstoy, Pushkin, Pasternak and Dostoevsky. Many of the courses in Ukrainian universities were taught in Russian. Since the collapse of the Soviet Union in 1991, the Ukrainian identity has slowly been evolving and strengthening. The Russian invasion of 2022 has supercharged this pride.

A strong sense of Ukrainian identity was surging through almost everyone we spoke to, fuelling the emotional fire to keep going, to keep pushing, to stay strong as the war drags on, year after year. Russia and Ukraine used to be uneasy neighbours, but now one party had tried to kill the other. The two countries may share a border 2000 kilometres long and have centuries of intertwined history, but in this case, blood is not thicker than water.

We never expected Ukrainians to wish their Russian blood relatives dead. But during our time in Ukraine, we came to understand the subterranean resentment, sometimes hatred, between many Russians and Ukrainians that this war exposed. We were shocked by the bluntness that we sometimes heard. One such conversation came in a café in Kyiv one afternoon where we were sitting at a table in the sun next to a couple in their twenties. Sylvie and I asked them for directions to the nearest computer shop and we began a conversation. It soon turned to the war, as conversations in Ukraine often do. The woman explained that this war had highlighted the sometimes difficult reality that many Ukrainians had Russian relatives. Over decades there has been so much intermarriage that this is common.

'I hope my Russian relatives get killed,' she says.

We thought we must have misheard her. 'Sorry?' we ask.

'I hope my Russian relatives get killed,' she repeats.

'Why?'

'Because they are Russians, and Russians have done nothing to stop this war.'

We say that it might be very difficult for people in Russia to do anything given the dictatorial nature of the regime.

'There are things that everyone can do,' she says. 'There would be all sorts of creative things they could do, and they don't even try. And what about all the Russians who live overseas? Where are the demonstrations? Where is there any support for us?'

We could understand the depth of hatred that many Ukrainians feel towards the Russians. Thousands of their fellow citizens had been killed or injured and their economy and livelihoods battered. But we also understood that on the Russian side, it might not be as simple as Ukrainians think it is to speak out. Inside Russian borders, there is an internal pressure that is hard for anyone to imagine. The Astra news service – a credible agency run by Russians who had to leave their country to be able to continue their reporting – discovered that there were at least fifteen sites in occupied Ukraine where Russians who refused to serve in the army were detained. There are multiple reports of many of these prisoners being tortured and denied food and water.

As a Russian-educated but Ukrainian-born journalist living in Ukraine, Yulia Eidel found herself in an odd position at the start of the war. As the Meduza website[8] reported, standing on the balcony of her apartment in Dnipro, one of Ukraine's largest cities close to Russia, she was near enough to the fighting to hear explosions in the distance as Russian artillery was fired towards a nearby airport.

Yulia was of the view that the war could be headed off if a critical mass of sane people in Russia applied enough pressure on their government. With this in mind, she wanted to see whether the students she studied journalism with at Moscow State University would join her in beginning an internet campaign for peace. Meduza reported that after fleeing Dnipro with her three children and arriving in the safety of a quiet village, Yulia sat at her computer and reached out to her former colleagues, telling them she now lived in Ukraine. 'Guys, you probably know, though you may have forgotten, that I'm originally from Ukraine. All of this is happening to me right now.' Yulia was concerned that there seemed little pushback to the Russian invasion from her former journalism school colleagues. She said that what she was trying to say to the other students was 'Let's come up with a solution together. What are you so silent for?'

Yulia was surprised by the resistance she faced. 'That situation isn't that simple,' one old student friend wrote. Another asked her not to turn their university chat group into 'a war-centric group'. But then one of the former students gave a much shorter response: 'Good evening.' That prompted another to reply, 'Well, here we go.'

According to Meduza, the student who said 'good evening' was Vladimir Tabak, the man who formed the Russian government's most effective social media network, known as Dialog, and part of Putin's propaganda machine. Yulia – who had not followed Tabak's career and was therefore mystified by the deadening effect his 'good evening' had on the chat group – privately messaged another of the former students to make inquiries. The reply was clear: 'He's one of the people who monitor social media groups and pages and report who should be shut down and who should receive support,' said her friend.

So the seeds of distrust were sown in the chat group. And it worked. Fearful of retribution, even while living in Ukraine, Yulia scaled back her comments to the group – avoiding saying anything that could compromise anyone – and slowly moved to other groups she felt she could trust more. Fear won.

For those in Yulia's chat group still living in Russia, they were also experiencing a different kind of punishment. While

Putin sat on his billions – evidence to the US Senate in 2017 estimated his wealth at A$275 billion, making him one of the world's richest people – for ordinary Russians, the first year of the invasion came with crippling sanctions of technological products, motor vehicles and medical equipment as countries reduced or cut exports to Russia altogether. But all these goods were still available if you knew the right person to ask. Reuters reported that while top brands pulled out of Russia, their goods remained easy to find: 'Trucks carrying Coca Cola roll across the border into Russia, tourists return from abroad laden with Zara's latest designs, and local online marketplaces snap up IKEA's furniture stocks … the main change has been to supply routes, but the products remain available both online and in stores. Buyers just need to know where to look.'[9]

Over time, Russia has largely managed to circumvent these sanctions, with particular help from Türkiye, which buys goods on Russia's behalf and then transports them across the border. While exports to Russia fell from many countries, exports from Türkiye grew an estimated forty per cent. Türkiye was therefore crucial as a sanctions buster.

Russia minimised the impact of sanctions through various complex international networks. The Carnegie Endowment for International Peace think-tank reported that both Moscow and its most important ally, Beijing, had shown they were capable of adapting to evolving sanctions: 'When leading

Chinese banks stopped dealing with Russian clients over the threat of secondary sanctions, regional banks stepped up to take their place. Schemes with numerous intermediaries from places such as Kazakhstan and the UAE also began to be used more actively, and companies began to use cryptocurrencies in payments. Bartering is also now flourishing, with Russian products exchanged for Chinese goods, eliminating the need for any bank transaction at all.'[10]

Carnegie noted that new sanctions introduced in June 2024 would have more bite than previous sanctions but were probably too little too late: 'The Russian government and businesses have been in survival mode ever since the start of the war, and devising various ways to keep doing business under ever stricter sanctions has become part of everyday life … in the two and a half years of war, an entire infrastructure of intermediaries in various jurisdictions has sprung up, schemes for swiftly restoring supply chains interrupted by sanctions have been developed, and payments in yuan and rubles have been settled using local infrastructure.' They conclude that it's too late to make an impact; this level of sanctioning needed to happen at the start of the war, not now. Therefore, everyday Russian life wasn't changing all that much.

Far more tragically than any inconvenience from sanctions, Russians have paid for Putin's war with their lives. In my visits to Ukraine, I saw many dead Russians – in photographs, at least.

Ukrainian soldiers would frequently show me pictures they'd taken on their phones at the front line. Part of the insidiousness of war is that it can normalise horror, and that seems to have happened with some Ukrainian soldiers I met. They would sometimes want to show me photos that, before the war began, they probably would have been horrified by. But as the war ground on, these photos were no longer regarded as shocking.

It wouldn't feel normal for the people who knew these soldiers. Looking at some of these dead young men whose bodies were in a state of decay, I couldn't help but think these were the sons, nephews, friends, colleagues and boyfriends of people back in Russia. They would be devastated if they had to see the photos I was looking at. Hopefully they would remember these young men as they had been when they last walked out the door. To draw on the famous Anzac prayer, it's we who are left who grow old.

This, however, is not how Anastasiia Lebedenko sees it. Like nearly everyone I interviewed in Ukraine, Anastasiia had a few choice words to say to the Russians: 'Go fuck yourselves.' This feeling extends not just to the soldiers who are devastating her country but to all Russians, who she sees as being mute pawns in the war happening on their border. 'Ukrainians tried to say a lot, especially in the first few months. They literally begged people to stand up, they begged them to come out to protest, they begged them to say something about this injustice. And what so many Russian people did was just ignore it and sit silently. I think this is also what makes us different.'

Anastasiia has little sympathy for our suggestion that it could be difficult for Russians to publicly stand against the war. 'First, I would make the comparison between them and so many other nations who are also enslaved by their corrupted leaders,' she says, 'and *they* chose to stand up and to say what they want to say and to stand for the values that are right for them.' She describes how, when she was working in Europe, she watched Iranian citizens protest against the water shortages back in Iran. But in the month she remained in Italy after the war broke out, she didn't see any protests by Russians against the war in Ukraine, despite them being in 'the safety of Europe, not in danger of the Russian police state'. 'I don't see them protesting, I don't see them doing anything. So for me, it all goes to show that all they care about is themselves.'

Across the country, Ukrainians are furious that anti-authoritarian Russians aren't standing up for the war crimes happening across their border. They are outraged.

One woman who doesn't share this view is Krystyna Orlova. We meet her through the break-dancing solider we watched during the street party at the start of this chapter. The soldier spoke little English, and Krystyna, standing nearby in the crowd and seeing that we are having trouble communicating, offers to assist with translation. This has been the way so much of our time in Ukraine has gone – we go with the flow. Wanting to talk to a dancing soldier leads us to spend the following day with Krystyna, her husband, David, and her three-year-old daughter, Yeva, and learn more about Ukrainians.

'We are very proud of our armed forces of Ukraine,' she tells us. 'All the time we're praying that they return alive and healthy. We are trying to do specific things which individual soldiers may ask for – if, for example, a soldier asks for tactical glasses or a specific brand of boots that he finds comfortable, we will buy them.'

Despite all the talk of a possible war, Krystyna says that she and her friends were shocked when the invasion occurred. 'We could not believe it when we saw the tanks rolling in – how could they come? We're an independent country.' She shows us a video of Yeva in bed, covering her ears to try to block the sound of air-raid sirens.

Despite the psychological and physiological warfare of the Russians, Krystyna has some empathy for everyday citizens in Russia. '[My view] is not very popular in Ukraine,' she explains, 'but I would tell [the Russians] that I understand they are living under a dictator and that things are difficult. If you have a child, you cannot go and protest because you could go to prison, and your child could be put in an institution for children without parents.' She gives the example of how a young girl in Russia made a drawing against the war and her father was sent to prison. As she didn't have a mother around, she was put into a home 'for children who are alone'. 'So I can't say to Russians, "Go and protest."'

Krystyna maintains this view despite her house in Mariupol being destroyed early in the war. The Siege of Mariupol was one of the earliest and bloodiest battles of the war. Russian forces targeted it soon after they crossed into Ukraine in February 2022. In their attack, according to United Nations estimates, Russian soldiers destroyed or damaged about ninety per cent of the residential buildings. After three months, Russia took control of Mariupol.

Krystyna and her husband had a beautiful house near the city's famous drama theatre. The family fled before Russian soldiers came and destroyed it, and when she saw for the first time a photograph of her destroyed home, she tells us, 'My heart was totally broken.' Mariupol, she adds, was an 800-year-old city with magnificent parks, a US-style playground and many facilities for families.

But despite what the Russian army did to her home, she still didn't give up on them as a people – at least, not at first. She says that because many Ukrainians have close family members in Russia, when the war started, President Zelensky asked them to start speaking with their Russian relatives to give them truthful information about the war. So she tried. 'I talked to them about the rockets, how our children are having to go to bunkers, about how thousands of Russian soldiers are dying,' she says. 'But they can't even feel our pain. Talking to my family members in Russia had zero effect. That is why there is no longer any dialogue between Ukrainians and their relatives in Russia.'

While Russia and Ukraine were once seen to share some joint history, those ties have been broken. But it's not just political and family bonds that have been broken – a common language has been cut down too. Families are no longer speaking, and many Ukrainians have stopped speaking Russian. It is an irony that Vladimir Putin launched his invasion to try to extend Russian influence but now, as a result of his actions, dramatically fewer people in Ukraine speak Russian than had previously.

Anastasiia's friend Olena, a 24-year-old graphic designer and illustrator, typifies many young Ukrainians: having grown up in a Russian-speaking family and educated primarily in Russian, she now prefers to speak Ukrainian. 'I did not speak Ukrainian until last year,' she says. 'But now I have switched from Russian to Ukrainian because it gives me so much empowerment.'

During Ukraine's seventy years of Soviet occupation, the official language was Russian. It was used by all government institutions, schools, universities and state media. Some families continued to speak Ukrainian at home, but when they were in public it was understood that people would switch to Russian. At shopping centres and on public transport, almost everybody spoke Russian. So for those who switched to speaking Ukrainian in public, it has been an active choice of defiance.

Olena says that until the invasion, many of her peers thought it was okay to speak Russian. But beyond that, she says, it was normal for Ukrainians to feel 'lesser than' Russians when compared to their neighbours. 'It was okay to think that our culture was not good enough, not as cool as Russian, for example,' she says. 'We had this thing that we were not as cool, that we were the smaller brother. But now we understand that we have our culture, we have our history, we have our strong ground and establishment here, and that we have what it takes to fight.'

Ukrainians know Russians better than anyone. They have lived alongside Russia and Russians and seen all sides of the Russian psyche. They know the long-held hostility that many Russians feel towards Ukrainians, how many look down on them. They heard Russians saying for decades that Ukraine is not a real country; that it doesn't really have its own culture. And now it is time to take their own back.

As someone who grew up with Russian films and books, Olena wants to explain to us Ukraine's new reality of war with its neighbour. To do this she points to a Soviet movie about a cat called Leopold. Leopold was a kind cat, but there were two mice who made his life a misery, destroying his house, destroying everything they could. Yet Leopold smiled at them and told them it was okay.

'But it's not okay,' says Olena. 'If these Russian destroyers come to our house, we can't be smiling and saying it's okay. We are fighters for our home and for our safety and for our culture. We are not Leopold!'

'So Ukrainians are no longer smiling cats?' we ask.

'No way, because we have been smiling cats for too long – now we are cats that can show our claws.'

At a personal level, Olena says the war has changed how she thinks about her own life. 'I have become more aware that I have only one life and that I need to make more conscious choices of how to live it.' Before the invasion, she says she felt young and like there was an endless number of opportunities and choices before her. But sometimes, she tells us, a person may not be able to decide what to do or which direction to take, so they just wait. 'When the war came, I realised that there is no time to wait,' she says. 'We will not live for thousands of years: we have this day, tomorrow, this week. I realised that I need to value this more, and value the people that I surround myself with and also what I am doing with my life. Do I like my work? Do I like my friends? My family? Of course you do, but you must ask yourself if you *love* your life.'

Even though Olena is living in a warzone, it's *her* warzone. Any sense of Russian comradeship has been destroyed. While Ukraine used to feel like the scorned, weaker sibling living in fear of their older bullying brother, they have now grown up and stood up for themselves.

So is it cool to be Ukrainian now? 'Yes, I am very proud!' Olena says. 'Being Ukrainian now is knowing who you are, knowing your strength. I am honestly scared on the inside. But you think, let's be peaceful, be kind. We have shown to the world that we are a kind people. Kindness is a good thing, but also knowing your worth is important. It should be connected. If you are just kind to everyone, they will bury you. They will fight your husband, they will fight your wife, they will take your home. They will take everything because you are kind to them, if you don't also have strength.'

We ask Olena what gives her strength. 'You feel stronger if you know who you are; that we have centuries of culture,' she says. 'We have our songs, our music, our national clothes. It's such a beautiful and important concept to have and understand that we have our history of Ukraine. Ukraine was not built as this little brother of Russia. No – we were founded before Russia existed. We are stronger now and more confident.'

CHAPTER 4

Medical marvels

As Russian soldiers cross the Ukrainian border on 24 February 2022, a separate and dramatic operation begins: an attempt to locate and rescue thousands of 'trapped' embryos and hundreds of distressed surrogate mothers. One of the key players in this extraordinary drama is working around the clock in a small office on Sydney's North Shore.

As director of Growing Families, a surrogacy support service, Sam Everingham has been working through the night. His organisation has been associated with Ukraine since 2016, helping Australians whose best chance of having a child is through a surrogate.

Ukraine has become one of the world's surrogate baby superpowers. For parents in countries around the globe experiencing difficulty having a child, they've frequently found themselves turning to 'the Ukraine solution'. Ukraine has become the new global hub of embryo transfer and surrogacy parenthood due to their large population and cultural acceptance of surrogacy and good invitro-fertilisation (IVF) facilities. In recent years, business has been booming. Per capita, Australia, China and Israel are the major clients of Ukraine's surrogacy services, and Growing Families has been the go-to organisation for hopeful parents in Australia, the US, France, Germany, Portugal, Romania, Australia, Belgium, Bulgaria, Norway, the Philippines, South Korea, Spain and Türkiye.

Ukraine's share of the international surrogacy market was boosted when Thailand, India, Nepal and Cambodia banned the industry because of the complications and risks that it brought. But thousands of Ukrainian women were willing to carry the fertilised eggs of foreign women in return for what, by Ukrainian standards, was a large amount of money. The entire process could cost a couple in Australia as much as AU$100,000, with surrogate mothers being paid on average US$12,000 to $15,000 to carry a child to birth. Some of these women will, over several years, carry two or three children for overseas clients.

'Before the Russian invasion, we were sending a lot of Australian couples there,' says Sam Everingham when I meet him in his Crows Nest office. He tells me that a large number of Americans couldn't afford surrogacy in the US, so they turned to Ukraine, which was a third of the price. Aside from the lower cost, it was also faster. In Australia the average wait time to find a surrogate is three to four years as the pool is so small, so a lot of Australians also turned to Ukraine in desperation.

They might have failed at IVF, have a debilitating illness or had their uterus removed. Typically, a couple makes their embryos in Australia and then sends them overseas to be implanted in Ukraine. 'In some cases they had no more eggs, so needed an egg donor *and* a surrogate,' Everingham explains, 'so we would ship the man's sperm to Ukraine.'

When Russia invaded Ukraine in 2022, Vladimir Putin unleashed chaos on thousands of intending parents around the world and the surrogates working with them. He threw a multi-million-dollar industry of embryos into disarray, both those sitting on ice in hospitals across the country as well as those growing inside surrogates. Many were within days of giving birth, setting off panic among both the surrogates as well as parents overseas. They had been getting monthly updates but now faced the prospect of being denied access not only to their surrogate but also to the newborn for whom they had waited so long.

When the Ukraine war began, Everingham's phone went into overdrive. Intending parents who had been paying large amounts of money to Ukrainian women carrying their embryos wanted to get their surrogates to safety. Growing Families was the only 'concierge support service' specialising in everything from helping parents navigate Covid-related travel lockdowns, to advising on reliable clinics in Ukraine, to helping with the paperwork that allows a newborn child to achieve citizenship, to securing travel documents for both baby and parents. And now he had to work out how to get unborn embryos, pregnant surrogates and newborn infants out of a warzone.

Dramatic rescue plans that are known in the security business as 'extractions' were put into action, but these were not just extracting adults or children but surrogates, newborns and embryos stored in icy liquid nitrogen. One embryologist was so concerned that Kyiv might fall that he packed thousands of carefully labelled embryos in liquid nitrogen into the boot of his car and drove them to the safety of Slovakia.

This gave rise to all sorts of diplomatic and ethical quandaries. If an Australian infant and their parents were stuck in a warzone, it would be the responsibility of the government to try to get them out, but did that also apply to a baby recently birthed by a Ukrainian woman, with Australian citizens for parents and no citizenship or passport? What about a frozen embryo, which is technically a bundle of Australian cells? What if that embryo is the *only* chance an Australian couple ever has of having a child – a child who will grow up to be an Australian citizen?

When news came through of the Russian invasion, Everingham worked through the night. One of the first things he did was to compile several lists: one for intending parents who had been able to contact their pregnant surrogate, one for those who had not been able to contact their surrogate, one for those who were in touch with their surrogacy agency, one for those who could not contact their surrogacy agency and one for those whose agency had simply vanished as the war began.

Everingham and others then began trying to contact officials with whom he'd had dealings as well as hospitals in Ukraine. He began running emergency webinars for intending parents around the world who had contacted him for information. He spoke to extraction teams with staff on the ground in Ukraine who might be able to help, and used his networks to recruit Ukrainians who had been surrogates in the past, hoping they might have information about current surrogates. The crisis was particularly acute in Kharkiv, which was under heavy Russian shelling.

Overnight, Everingham had to become part travel agent, part crisis manager, part consular assistant and part psychologist. He contacted security firms in the US and Australia who specialised in international evacuations. But many clients could not afford the thousands of dollars it would cost to do a high-end extraction of their surrogate in an armoured vehicle. So Everingham tracked down and translated bus and train schedules around Ukraine to help expectant women find escape routes. And through all of this, he needed to try to keep both intending parents and surrogates calm.

An email that one Australian couple sent him in 2022 illustrated the typical concerns:

Hi Sam,

Thank you so much for that webinar and your help more widely, it's incredibly generous.

Our surrogate is twenty weeks pregnant and in the Obolon district of Kyiv. We have direct contact with her and will get more specific details as she has moved to a bunker. She has her seven-year-old son with her.

We would be extremely keen to have her be part of any evacuation plans as a group, or singly.

We have mentioned evacuation to her (and sent her money to support it) and she is quite scared that the rest of Ukraine might be equally unsafe – we have not pushed on this, though we feel strongly she should move. We feel that clear information about the potential for transport, by who, and her opportunity to access accommodation and services in Lviv or Vinnytsia, or across the border, would be extremely valuable. We would deeply appreciate any local language help in explaining the practicalities and potential benefits of a move if you could help organise that.

Please let us know next steps and how we can help.

Deepest thanks,

(name withheld for privacy reasons)

The first on-the-ground priority was to keep in contact with surrogates and get them to safety. But communication was erratic, with phone services and internet access crashing due to the overload that the outbreak of war was causing. The next challenge was to try to connect surrogates with intending parents across international borders. Given the fear and unpredictability inside Ukraine, many surrogates were afraid to travel. They were particularly resistant to leaving Ukraine in case they could not return. Growing Families found people able to speak to surrogates and talk them through the process. Safe houses were set up outside Kyiv, away from the shelling and en route to the border with Poland. From these, surrogates and newborns were united with volunteer or paid evacuation teams who could take them to the border or safer cities.

But understandably, many surrogates did not want to be separated from their own families. As part of Ukraine's response to war, Volodymyr Zelensky had ruled that all men from eighteen to sixty could not leave Ukraine in case they were needed to go to the front. Stories started circulating of fighting-age civilian males being shot as deserters if they approached the border. Many surrogates therefore refused to try to cross the border with their husbands; if they had already given birth, sometimes they would take the newborn close to the border and ask the intended parents to cross into Ukraine from Poland to collect them. 'She'd say, "Here's the baby, I'm staying in Ukraine,"' Everingham says.

Even when extraction plans were successfully made, many women were too scared to leave their places of safety to meet at organised checkpoints. 'It was a nightmare,' Everingham says. He describes one case where a surrogate was supposed to be picked up in Kyiv to be taken to the border, 'and for some reason she wasn't at the pick-up point,' he says. 'I think at one stage, both me and the security agency director were yelling at each other because we were so stressed out.' On another occasion Everingham had the intending parent on the phone to the surrogate, trying to convince her to leave for the meeting point. But the surrogate kept asking, 'Can I be sure to get to the meeting point safely?' The would-be parents were concerned about the safety of their unborn children, but the women carrying their babies were also concerned for their own lives.

Even if they could get a surrogate to the border, the issues didn't stop there. The outbreak of war always causes a rush on borders so already there were thousands of Ukrainians and foreigners trying to flee. When the war broke out, many government agencies in Ukraine descended into chaos or closed as men headed to the front line and some women and children tried to leave the country. Surrogates who had recently given birth therefore began turning up at the border with babies who had no paperwork, not even a birth certificate.

Foreign couples who had entered Ukraine against the advice of their own governments hours or days before to collect their surrogate children were now trying to leave with a third person – their new baby. Trying to navigate a foreign border without speaking the language was difficult enough, but the task was made vastly more difficult with an undocumented infant. As far as the border guards were concerned, these foreigners may have been child trafficking. To get around this new complication, Growing Families advised surrogates to record video messages explaining that they had carried the babies to birth and then willingly handed them over to the parents as part of a surrogacy agreement. It was enough to convince some Ukrainian border guards to let this suddenly expanded family leave the country.

As the weeks passed and couples started taking more risks, it became clear that there had been Ukrainian agencies working with same-sex couples for surrogacy, something that is illegal in Ukraine. One such French couple was arrested and prosecuted in Lviv while trying to retrieve their newborn.

Another complication was that for many surrogates about to give birth, the closest hospitals outside Ukraine were in Poland, a country that is traditionally opposed to surrogacy. 'We had to tiptoe around that issue with the hospitals,' Everingham says. 'We had to pretend the surrogate was the mother because Poland is very Catholic. We were faced with the reality that we had all these Ukrainian surrogates arriving in Warsaw who spoke no Polish and knew no-one there, so we had to give them whatever support we could.'

One of the most dramatic cases involved intending parents Sungsil and Kyung from South Korea. As Everingham wrote later in his book *Surrogacy Stories*,[11] Sungsil knew from the age of eighteen that she was not able to carry a child. Twelve years after creating and freezing a dozen embryos, only four of which turned out to be viable, she and Kyung sought a surrogate mother in Ukraine. Their surrogate, Maryina, lived outside Kyiv with her husband and two children and was thirty-eight weeks pregnant when the war broke out.

> For Maryina the decision was agonising … her own
> children were at home more than three hours southeast
> [of Kyiv] and the evacuation team had no means to
> collect them en route … A Geneva-based non-government
> organisation working with Growing Families found a
> seat on a humanitarian train organised by the Polish
> government. It would depart Kyiv's main station for
> Warsaw in just three and a half hours and would be at
> least a fifteen-hour journey.
>
> A Ukraine translator was called in to explain the
> option to Maryina. If she went, she needed to get to the
> station, find platform 14, call a co-ordinator and provide
> a password: PKP Intercity … Sungsil and Kyung [in

South Korea] booked their flight to Warsaw along with
a hotel room near Warsaw's train terminus for Maryina.
They still had no idea where Maryina would give birth,
assuming she did not go into labour and birth their child
in transit.

At Warsaw's main station it was chaos. Unable to get
a response via WhatsApp – Maryina had no internet
connection and her Ukraine number would not work in
Poland – Sungsil's Warsaw contact stood on one of the
seats on the platform and yelled out Maryina's name.
It was useless amid all the noise. They tried asking
disembarking passengers if they had seen a pregnant
woman on the train. Some in the crowd pointed towards
where they had seen a heavily pregnant woman, and
Maryina was finally located.

Sungsil and Kyung arrived in Warsaw late Monday
night but it was Tuesday morning before they finally
met Maryina face to face. Sungsil sobbed and hugged
this woman she had never met … two days later the trio
met with the Warsaw gynaecologist and his team at the
recommended hospital before returning to the hotel.
Sungsil and Kyung had been advised not to tell the
hospital about the surrogacy arrangement, so Sungsil
came up with a bizarre explanation: Maryina was her
friend and her own husband had fathered the child

Maryina carried. Sungsil was a forgiving friend and was there for support.

Maryina gave birth to a boy. They had already chosen the name Sean, which means 'gift from God' … It was two long days before Maryina and Sean were discharged, allowing Sungsil to hold her infant for the first time … holding their child 12 years after creating his embryos was a surreal feeling.

Maryina spent the next few weeks recuperating before moving into an apartment with Sungsil, Kyung and Sean. As they shared meals and days together, their understanding of each other deepened … Sungsil had plenty of time to reflect on her new life: 'Becoming Sean's mum changed everything – my perspective on life, work … I used to be a task-driven person, a bit of a workaholic and thriving to achieve something. Such [a] personality was okay for one season of my life and now I need to be more flexible and chilled out with Sean.'

Excerpted from *Surrogacy Stories*, by Sam Everingham and Kerry Duncan

Out of all of the death and tragedy of Vladimir Putin's war, some stories of joy and new life had emerged.

*

Two days before Russia's invasion of Ukraine, Dr Andrii Hanych, one of Ukraine's leading cancer doctors, left his hospital in Mariupol to get some fresh air. A reporter from the German news agency Deutsche Welle recognised him and approached him with a simple question: what will you do if Putin attacks? Dr Hanych replied that he would take up a weapon, even throwing explosives. 'We would take up rifles, throw Molotov cocktails at them. We will defend ourselves.'

The cancer doctor was confident that Putin would not invade. 'Deep in my soul I believed we had been so well prepared for the attack that the attack will not take place,' he later tells Paul Goldberg, who documented this story in *The Cancer Letter* publication.[12] 'It's hard to believe, but I simply didn't foresee it.'

Dr Hanych's optimism was misplaced. Not long after, he found himself sleeping in the hospital with twelve of his cancer patients. At first they used hospital beds, but then he realised it would make more sense to use infusion chairs. 'They are less comfortable but more convenient,' he said. 'If there is bombing on the side of the kitchen, you roll them to the opposite side.'

And so began the extraordinary story of how this 43-year-old doctor would try to continue the treatment of his cancer patients while war raged around them. Dr Hanych was chief of the radiation oncology department at the Municipal Interdistrict

Regional Oncologic Dispensary in Mariupol, a city that saw some of the worst fighting over many months between Russian and Ukrainian soldiers.

Goldberg wrote that Dr Hanych was inside the shrapnel-damaged building trying to keep the twelve patients alive amid whistling mortar shells and volleys of fire unleashed by Russian tanks.

> Cancer treatment in Mariupol became impossible as soon as the Russian invasion began on February 24. Electricity went out within a couple of days. Gas was turned off soon thereafter. Sirens blasted on the first day, maybe two, but sirens don't work in the absence of electricity. Besides, what use would anyone in Mariupol have for a siren? What can a siren accomplish in a city under attack? Help you realise that there is no safety? The 12 cancer patients in Hanych's care had a range of malignancies: brain tumours, breast cancer, head and neck cancer, colon cancer, lung cancer. They weren't Mariupol residents. They came from nearby villages and small towns. Advancing Russian troops deprived them of a place to return and Hanych had no choice but to become their caretaker of last resort.

The report said the hospital was empty of staff – it was just Dr Hanych and the twelve patients. He decided to sleep there.

He said later that he couldn't tell the patients to leave as they often no longer had a home to return to. Because the electricity was turned off, he would make trips when he could to his apartment to boil water on the gas stove to bring back to the hospital. To entertain the patients, in the evening he would play 'something happy' on his guitar. One of the patients with colon cancer came up to him and said, 'You know, doctor, I enjoyed this so much that my tumour has dissolved.'

While Dr Hanych tried to continue the treatment of the patients, horrors took place around the hospital. He recalled how one of the nurses borrowed a wheelchair to transport her eighty-year-old mother home. While the old woman's grandson was returning the wheelchair to the hospital for his mum, he witnessed a young man get blown apart in an explosion as the young man's mother watched in horror. She asked him for help gathering the pieces of her son's body, loading them onto the wheelchair and taking them to the courtyard of a residential building for burial. Even in the horrors of war, the woman wanted to give her son a dignified burial.

When the war began, Dr Hanych believed that the Russians would not bomb a hospital complex. How wrong he was. On 1 March 2022, a missile hit a transformer station that was alongside the radiation therapy department, not far from Dr Hanych and his patients. 'If they drop one bomb, you know they will drop another,' he said, 'When you realise that, all your illusions vanish.'

With Russian soldiers getting closer and closer, everyone agreed it was time for the patients to be evacuated. Ukrainian soldiers helped them to leave. Then Dr Hanych and five others – medical staff and family members – also decided to leave. 'I wasn't thinking about leaving at first,' he says later. 'But shooting intensified day by day, mortars whistled every minute. You pray that they fly by, but then you realise that if they fly by you, they may hit someone else. Then Russian tanks started to appear.'

Dr Hanych's group got five hundred metres from the hospital and encountered mortar fire so ran to a bomb shelter. The group then got to the limestone cliffs of the Sea of Azov. They turned and looked back at Mariupol. 'It's a terrifying sight,' Dr Hanych says. 'We see smoke rise. Black smoke coming from many, many places. This is something I cannot put into words.'

He had a realisation that his new life was beginning, but he didn't know what that new life would be. 'None of us know where we are going. None of us know what's going on in Ukraine. Has Kyiv fallen? Nothing is known,' he says. 'Absolutely nothing, just an indescribable euphoria, an apocalyptic euphoria.'

As the group walked along a deserted beach, they saw a Russian plane. They learned later that it bombed the Donetsk Academic Regional Drama Theatre in Mariupol. As Paul Goldberg writes in the conclusion to this essay: 'As many as 600 people, children among them, will die in that rubble, and another item will be added to the list of Russia's crimes against humanity.'

*

I am standing in a room filled with dozens of human body parts: forearms, shoulder sockets, calves capped off at the knee. But these limbs are not made of flesh and bone but titanium, silicone and thermoplastics.

Dr Andrii Palamarchuk started this rehabilitation clinic in May 2022, three months after the Russian invasion. To begin with, the clinic offered physiotherapy, physical therapy, medication treatment and psychological support. In its first weeks the clinic had four patients and a staff of three. Within a year it had a staff of twenty-four and more than forty patients each day, mainly wounded soldiers. Dr Palamarchuk reinvented himself from a rehabilitation doctor to one who had to run a business too, effectively becoming an entrepreneur with as much of an eye on donations to fund his new clinic as healthcare.

The growth of the clinic, including the purchase of the best rehabilitation equipment, was due to funding from the United Ukraine Appeal in Australia. Ukrainian fundraisers spend much of their time working with international groups to bankroll the war. Dr Palamarchuk says without the money from Australia's Ukrainian community, the clinic would not be operating.

Funding for the clinic extends to prosthetics, the expertly made replacements for lost arms or legs. Tragically, prosthetics have become one of the grim boom industries of this war. The funding for this clinic ensured that Ukraine could make its own prosthetics for its growing demand rather than import them. Dr Palamarchuk says the number of people needing rehabilitation grew some four hundred per cent within a year of the war. However, the mental health toll is incalculable. 'It could take ten years to assess the true damage of the war,' he says. 'The country faces a huge upswing in psychological problems.'

Many of the Ukrainians with whom Sylvie and I spoke said the war had changed them. This became a theme we would explore with almost everyone we met. 'If I compare myself before the war and during the war, I see for myself that I've changed my view of the world,' Dr Palamarchuk says. He's changed the way he talks to patients, particularly soldiers. Part of that change is that now he attempts to communicate using more humour – he believes this helps to lift the spirits of patients. He says he's also learnt from the strength of young people. 'The young people teach me about the future of my country. Before I didn't see the great future which I see right now. I hope that these young strong people will help to grow another society [after the war].'

I spend an afternoon in this clinic, where I meet young Ukrainian men trying to rebuild their lives after being injured on the front line. Oleg Tyzch, twenty-nine, was already in the army when Russia invaded and was sent to fight in Luhansk on the country's far eastern border. As he tries to stretch his injured leg, he tells me that he was in a trench when a Russian shell landed near him, smashing the bones from his right hip to his knee. When he arrived at the clinic he was in a wheelchair. After a month of therapy, his pride is obvious as he explains to me that he can walk again, albeit with the help of crutches.

Fireman Andrii Vovchuk is another person at the clinic trying to rebuild his life. On 19 March 2022, he was called to a fire on the outskirts of Kyiv. Russian soldiers were still in the outer suburbs, having not yet been fully repelled. As the Russians were in retreat, they buried landmines in the roads. Andrii and his crew were rushing to a fire when their truck ran over one. His legs were blown off.

In one of the upstairs rooms of the clinic I find Andrii managing to lift himself out of his chair. With the help of crutches and prosthetics, he's able to walk again. As I watch him, I'm in awe of his determination. It is a privilege to witness his joy – the sort of delight we've seen in videos that show the sheer amazement of a deaf child suddenly able to hear, or a sight-impaired child given their first glasses. Today, with tenacity and focus, Andrii is able to take six or seven steps. He then needs to rest as he's short of breath, but he's very pleased with his progress. If he can take two or three more steps each day, that is real progress of which he can be proud. Being able to walk again gives him a clear sense of achievement.

Traveling around wartime Ukraine, it becomes clear that everything in life is relative. When I first look at Andrii, I see a man with no legs. But when he looks at himself, he sees a man learning to walk again, making progress day by day. I realise as I sit talking to him that his perspective is so much better than mine. I need to take more pleasure out of every little victory, simple pleasures and achievements in life such as walking, breathing and sleeping. Andrii has a physical limitation; I have a mindset limitation. He is dealing with his limitation – I should deal with mine.

Nonetheless, the physical cost of this war is confronting. Wherever you go in Ukraine you see the walking wounded. One Friday night, as Sylvie and I walk near one of the major metro stations, we come across 23-year-old Maks Filatov. Maks was already in the army when the war began and quickly found himself facing Russia's soldiers. A mortar exploded nearby, smashing his lower leg. He spent months going to medical appointments but was making little progress. The Ukrainian army decided that a specialist in Germany was the best hope for him, so he moved there for treatment. On return, with his leg in slow recovery and unable to rejoin to the front line, he joined Ukraine's huge volunteer army.

Maks' new role in life is to be a comfort to others who are injured. He spends his days going to hospitals visiting injured soldiers. He takes them food, but the part of the job he finds most satisfying is simply spending time with them. His time and company are his gift, and they alone give him great pleasure. He tells us that if a patient wants to talk, he sits there and listens. If they want silence, he just sits with them in silence. His own dreadful injury led to a discovery.

'When I was in Germany in hospital, what I found hard was not just the pain but the fact that no-one ever visited me,' he says. 'So now I go to hospitals where people are injured and I bring them a bit of company, some sweets, some clothes or what I can afford on my salary. Sometimes we talk. Sometimes we stay quiet.

'The war taught me that there are different kinds of people,' he continues. 'There are bad ones, good ones … War made me understand that I do not have that much time. I understood that I had not lived much and that I wanted to have a family … I would even want to have children. The war made me more thoughtful. I now do not wish bad for anyone else. I now think that you should treat people how you would like them to treat you. I now believe that you should make more effort to be able to appreciate life.'

And so, at the age of twenty-three, Maks has discovered something new and important: that his company has a value. That *he* is valuable.

I, too, discovered many things in wartime Ukraine. A major revelation for me was that sometimes the most powerful insights of war come from children.

CHAPTER 5

Children of the war

IT'S SOMETIMES SAID THAT JOURNALISTS WRITE THE FIRST drafts of history. In Ukraine, one of those first drafts has been written by a remarkable eight-year-old boy. When Russia invaded, Yegor Kravstov and his family were living in Mariupol, a city that became the focus of international attention for one of the worst battles of the war. Yegor is the boy who rallied a country.

For ninety-six days, Yegor, his mother, sister and grandparents were trapped in their house, unable to leave as fighting raged around them. The electricity wasn't working, his phone had died and he had no internet. So Yegor decided to take up a pen and notepad and begin writing a diary. It is wonderful in its simplicity. 'I am eight, my sister is fifteen, my mum is thirty-eight,' he begins. Yegor goes on to record some of the desperation of the war. 'My two dogs have died and my neighbour next door has died.'

Parts of the diary began to be circulated on social media, where page after page was posted on Facebook and Instagram. Yegor's story mesmerised Ukrainians. One of Ukraine's most famous singers, Tina Karol, saw him on TV talking about his diary. She brought him along to one of her performances, and then, given that his family had lost their home, she bought them a new apartment.

As a journalist, you get to meet hundreds of interesting and delightful people (and sometimes less delightful ones). Yegor was a true gem, a boy with real presence and grace, particularly given the horrors he'd been through. In his diary, and in the hours I spent with him, he was able to articulate what he'd been through, as harrowing as it was.

As we sit in the sun on a park bench talking about his experiences, Yegor tells me that when he thinks about Mariupol, 'I only remember that everything was burnt, we had pieces of shells outside, and the city was burnt.'

A Russian shell had hit the family home, destroying much of the house and seriously injuring his grandfather. For three days his grandfather bled, but because of the battles outside, the family could not get him medical help. His grandfather died.

How does a child ever get over watching their grandfather bleed to death? How will the children of Ukraine recover from the trauma of this war?

Yegor's mother, Elena, says even though Tina Karol bought the family a new apartment well away from the front line, in Ukraine it's difficult to escape the war entirely. 'This apartment is near a power station, and some nights you can hear the Russian missiles trying to hit the station. We have not escaped the war completely.' I ask Elena what she thinks when she sees Vladimir Putin on television. 'I would like him to suffer, not just to die. I want him to suffer for a long time so that he can live through what we and everyone else has gone through.' She gives credit to Yegor and his sister, Veronka, for helping her to get through the dark days of the Siege of Mariupol. 'Thanks to them, we survived,' she says. 'I realised that I needed to live because of them, to keep them alive. In the very first days, I tried to make up stories that [the sounds of explosions] were fireworks and things, but they told me, "Mum, we are grown-ups, we know there are shootings outside."'

Yegor's life has been turned upside down by this war. He's lost his grandfather, his neighbour and several pets and had to flee from a city under siege to a new home on the other side of the country. The diary showed the great benefit of someone expressing their feelings on paper, but over my time with Yegor and his family, I also saw a real gentleness and generosity.

Beneath the gentleness there was a steely character. As we were winding up our chat, Elena pointed me to the last page of Yegor's diary. 'See the drawing of Putin?' she asked. I had not, so I turned to it. Yegor had drawn Vladimir Putin with a nuclear bomb hanging over his head and a maniacal grin on his face.

'Why is Putin smiling?' I ask.

With an impish grin, Yegor looked at his drawing of Putin then looked back at me. 'Because he's crazy.'

Yegor is extraordinary for his age – he has a quiet and dignified strength about him. I ask what message he might have for children in Australia, and his answer shows his generosity of character. He says it would be better if children in Australia did not know details about this conflict. He wants to spare them the horrors of war. But then after a pause, he adds, 'I wish them well and hope that they can fulfil their dreams.'

*

As I've seen in many of the conflicts that I've covered, children often absorb the horror of war more than anybody. Often they prefer not to talk about their experiences, but I've found that when they are prepared to discuss their lives, they give the most powerful accounts of the war.

Some extraordinary groups have emerged to support these children. One is Save Ukraine, an agency formed to retrieve children who have been taken from Ukraine to Russia or its occupied territories. Its twelve evacuation teams target different regions under Russian occupation and work with families to get their kids back. 'Save Ukraine is a rescue network,' says press officer Olga Yerokhina. 'We rescue people, restore and rebuild.'

I ask Olga if Russia has been stealing children. 'We don't call it by that word,' she says. 'We call it deportation, like displacement of our people ... It's part of a big policy of the state of Russia, when under the guise of evacuation or "rest or rehabilitation", they displace a whole group of children, families or people.'

If children are taken against their will, isn't that kidnapping? 'We can call it kidnapping,' Olga agrees. 'We can call these children abducted children or deported children.' She explains that according to international law, Russia must give Ukrainian officials lists of families or children who are displaced. But Russia isn't providing any such lists. 'So we don't know how many children are there, how many families are there for sure,' she says. 'We don't do any negotiations with [Russia] because we are at a state of war. We have no diplomatic relations with Russia – they should give us those lists, but it's not going to happen.'

Olga gives the example of a boy from Kharkiv, near the Russian border, who went to get his belongings from his school. Russians swept in and took him and other children from his school, put them into their cars and 'displaced' them into the so-called Luhansk People's Republic, which is part of occupied Russian territory. They moved him from one place to another. He was scared and wanted to go home, but his mother didn't know where he was.

It's a widely held view in Ukraine that Russia tries to indoctrinate Ukrainian children in Crimea and other occupied territories. Olga agrees. 'They are definitely trying to brainwash our children. Children have told us that they were forced to sing the [Russian] anthem, and some of them must do this four or five times a day.' She says that at these 'schools', Ukrainian children study Russian history and the Russian language. Save Ukraine has seized examples of their textbooks, where Ukraine is painted in a demonising light. 'The children who were a long time in this atmosphere start maybe to look differently on this whole situation,' Olga says, 'because it's very easy to have an influence on children.'

Save Ukraine works to prepare parents – usually mothers – to physically go to occupied territories to try to rescue their children. 'We prepare them that it will be a very long and hard trip because they will face a very difficult route,' Olga says. 'When these mothers are there and try to get back their children, Russian authorities don't help. Mothers basically need to walk their children out of the camps.'

I ask Olga whether Russia is trying to make these children permanently Russian. 'We think that Russia uses our children for propaganda purposes,' she says. 'They show the children photographs that glorify Russia and tell them that they have a bright future there.' One girl told Olga that the Russians offered to take her to the Ural region and promised to get her an apartment there in the future and give her money. They try to convince the children that they care about them. 'On the other side,' she says, 'they show these children that Ukraine is bad, that you don't have any future in Ukraine.'

Children who return home from these Russian schools informed Save Ukraine that they were told Ukraine didn't need them and that Ukraine was not a country. It was a part of Russia and 'all of you will be our citizens,' says Olga. 'So yes, we face this propaganda, this politics, and we must stand up against it.'

But it's not all happy reunion stories for Olga. Her agency was told the names of sixteen to eighteen Ukrainian children who are in Russian camps but have had no parents telephoning or trying to retrieve them. 'We haven't received any applications,' she says. 'We are concerned that no-one is looking for them.'

Her coworker Hannah suggests a sombre theory: 'Their parents could be dead.'

*

Fifteen-year-old Genia is one of the lucky children who was saved from a Russian camp in Crimea by her mother. The nightmare for Genia and her mother, Maryna, began in October 2022, eight months after Russia's invasion. They lived in Kherson, which Russian soldiers quickly overran, beginning a military occupation. So when the head teacher proposed that the whole class go on a 'rest and healing camp' for two weeks during school holidays, it seemed like a good idea. The fighting was in full flight, so many of the parents thought that it would be good for the children to get away from the war.

They found out that the school camp would be in Crimea only once arrangements had been made. But even that wasn't enough to set off alarm bells. Like much of the east along the border with Russia, the area around Kherson is Russian-speaking in large part, and it's not unusual for people from Russian-speaking parts of Ukraine to go on holidays to the Russian-occupied Crimean Peninsula. So Maryna bade her daughter farewell, thinking she would see her again in a fortnight.

Soon after Genia arrived in Crimea, things began to change. 'We were told that holidays in school had been extended for an unknown period,' Maryna says. 'And then they kept saying the same thing, which ended up being six months.' More odd things began to happen. The children were moved from one camp in Crimea to another. Different excuses were given for the moving of the children: organisers said they wanted to reduce the size of the groups, then on another occasion the excuse was a lack of heating.

Parents became alarmed. When Maryna, in a phone call, asked the head teacher – who had gone to Crimea with the children – why the school camp kept being extended, the teacher admitted that she knew from the beginning that it would not be a two-week trip to Crimea but at least three months. It would become obvious later that the head teacher at Genia's school was in league with the Russian occupiers, but this was not clear to Maryna and the other parents at the time.

Maryna was outraged and began calling other parents to try to work out what they should all do. Worse still, the teacher told Maryna that she was planning to remain in Crimea and start a new life there. Maryna later found out that the teacher's salary was doubled for taking the children to a Russian camp in Crimea. 'I think she did it just for her own wealth,' she says.

Genia described her experience at the camps for me. 'In the first camp, everything was fine,' she says. They'd exercise in the morning and eat breakfast, and in the afternoons they would have Russian language and history lessons alongside algebra and geometry, so there was a normalcy to the camp in terms of daily activities.

But things deteriorated markedly at the second location, which also housed Russian students. The hostility began from the moment Genia and the other Ukrainian children arrived. 'We were like in a prison,' she says. 'The very first day we were brought to the orientation meeting in a hall with a stage, and the director of the camp had a microphone and started to tell us that we were Nazis and fascists and other insults,' she recalls. Some of the Ukrainian children began shouting, 'Slava Ukraine!' ('Glory to Ukraine!') The director shouted back at them. Genia remembers him yelling, 'You don't have your own opinion. There is the right one, which is mine, and the wrong one, which is yours. You are here like in prison. So you will be doing what I tell you.'

'Then we got used to that,' Genia says simply.

They were then sent to a third camp in Yevpatoria in western Crimea where the pro-Russia propaganda really ramped up. At the morning assembly, the Ukrainian children were made to sing the Russian national anthem. On Russian national holidays, the children had to sing patriotic songs. Russian children came and later were allowed to return home, but the Ukrainian children were not allowed to go back to Ukraine.

So did Genia think she would ever see her mother again? 'We were told that we would never come back home – that unless your parents show up here, you will be sent to the orphan house. We thought that it's the end, we will never come back. We will never see anyone.'

Genia did whatever she could to survive in a hostile environment, but she felt the pressure to be indoctrinated into a Russian way of life. 'They wanted us to change who we are,' she says. '[The supervisors] were always wearing the Z symbol or patches on their shirts.' In Putin's Russia, the Z symbol is seen as the symbol of Russia. 'If they spotted us wearing Ukrainian flags or other symbols, they made us clean the camp or write a note to the management about why we were wearing Ukrainian symbols in Russia.'

The Ukrainian children maintained their low-level resistance. One day there was an event where there were many coloured balloons. Genia and one of the other Ukrainian children souvenired a yellow and a blue balloon, the colours of Ukraine's flag. 'We put them in our room on the wall, and then the deputy director came to our room and tore down the balloons,' she says. 'She shouted at us and said, "You don't respect our country. You drink our water and eat our bread and behave like that." She insulted us and walked away with our balloons.'

As to the invasion of Ukraine – which those in charge of the schools referred to by the approved description from Moscow as a 'special military operation' – Genia says the teachers who spoke at assembly would tell them, 'We are actually saving you.' In reality, it was Genia who needed saving from this anti-Ukrainian culture. Her mother back in Ukraine was working out a plan.

Genia had been sharing a room with another Ukrainian girl, and Maryna found out that the mother of that girl had been to Crimea and brought her back. 'I asked for that mother's phone number, and she gave me a number for Save Ukraine,' Maryna says. 'So I contacted them and then they organised a trip to get our children back.'

By the time Genia's mother came, she was the only Ukrainian child at Yevpatoria. 'I was very sad because I was alone there,' she says. 'When there were some other Ukrainian children at the camps, at least they were my friends. We had some fun. It happened suddenly that other Ukrainian children left and I was alone.' She tried being friends with some of the Russian children, but they were 'different'. She says some of them were kind, but others called her names.

The reunion with Genia was extraordinary. Once Maryna arrived at the camp – referred to by Russians as a 'sanatorium' – she asked the guard at the front gate if he could contact her daughter. '[Genia] was brought to the front gate by a nurse in a white uniform with a shopping bag with her things, and the nurse gave me a piece of paper to sign,' she remembers. No officials, no apology, just her child thrust back to her through the gate. She says children from windows were shouting, 'Genia! Genia!' It was the Russian children saying goodbye.

Maryna says if it had not been for Save Ukraine, she would not have been able to retrieve her daughter. For those parents who tried to do so independently, it was almost impossible. She said she'd heard the camp tried to convince some parents who'd gone to get their children that they should remain in

Crimea with their children. 'They were offering them official papers, and some of the parents made such decisions,' she says. 'Those parents who'd gone to get children on their own without Save Ukraine already knew that they were not coming back to Kherson. You could go to Crimea, but the questions would be, how are you going to get out of Crimea?'

*

For those parents who did make it out of Crimea with their children, it quickly became clear that some of the children were not well. I drive to a rehabilitation centre in Kyiv where children traumatised by this war come to work through their emotions using a creative tool: art therapy.

The classes take place in an old four-storey building that houses one of Save Ukraine's 'hope and healing centres'. In addition to helping parents bring their children home from occupied Russian territories, Save Ukraine has set up spaces across the country where traumatised women and children can stay while they're trying to get their lives in order. These include fifteen community drop-in centres for the children of displaced families to study and do activities such as art and dancing lessons. As I walk up to the top floor of this centre, I see several women cooking meals, doing washing or taking care of young children and babies. I see no men, presumably all off at the front line or at work.

As is typical in this country, there are plenty of staff and volunteers at this refuge who are as important to the war effort as the soldiers fighting the Russians.

Hanna Gorkun, the director of the centre, is typical – her focus is on helping these women and children who've been battered by war.

Hanna is keen to show me the art room, which is full of paintings and drawings. 'These are not just pictures, they're part of therapy,' she says. Children work in pairs under the supervision of an adult: one child lies down on the sheet of paper while the second child draws their outline, then they colour their own outline in. They're told to show how they see themselves from the outside. 'Aim number one is for a child to feel the emotions,' Hanna says. 'So they're asked what emotions they feel, for example, anger, sadness, happiness, fear. The next step is to allocate where these emotions are in their bodies: where does their fear live? Their anger? Their happiness?'

Children then paint the emotions they feel where they feel them in their bodies. 'For example, a child may say they feel happiness in their lips, a smile,' Hanna says. 'Anger in her legs. Or anger in her hands when she clenches her fist.' The children are also given stickers on which they can write anything they think is relevant to explaining how they are feeling or what they see as their way of handling their emotions. Through this exercise, Hanna encourages the children not only to feel their emotions but name and work through them. As therapists, Hanna and her colleagues try to stand back and let the children take control of the exercises. 'It doesn't matter where they say they feel the emotions,' she explains. 'It's a device to get them to start talking about their emotions rather than keeping them all to themselves. Having to talk about their emotions to another child is important.'

Hanna takes me to a corner of the main art room and directs me to a particular painting. 'On this picture you can see on one of the girl's green hands she's written on a sticker "dancing", and she said that laughing is how she expresses her happiness,' she explains. On another painting, a child has written on a sticker 'Kill Putin'. Another child has drawn herself stamping her feet, which she told the therapist was a way for her to get over her anger. She also wrote 'go for a walk' and 'want to kill everyone' as reactions to anger. On another piece of butcher paper the therapist has asked, 'To whom can I turn in order to receive love?' One child has placed a sticker with 'my father' under the question, while another has written 'my friend'.

'This is all about how to teach children to help themselves get over this state of being under pressure,' says Hanna. 'To help the children feel alive and able to find resources which can help in difficult situations. The key themes we want to help them [with] are working out to whom they can turn, who can comfort them?

How can you help yourself? It's about how a child understands themselves in this situation and can help themselves.'

One of the most revealing parts of this art therapy is the section where paintings have been divided into those done by children before they have received any counselling and those after. One of the hallmarks of the 'before' drawings, says Hanna, is that often a child is thinking only about surviving. 'Before any therapy, the children who come in here are usually very serious and self-focused. Some can show no emotion. It can be scary when children come in here and are very serious. When children are starting to make a mess, I'm very happy that they behave like children.'

One of the 'before' drawings depicts a school being attacked by tanks, shells and rockets. The school is drawn with red paint, which the child told the therapist was to represent blood. Another 'before' drawing has a house being hit by a rocket. The house is on fire. Planes with 'Ukraine' written on them are flying towards the house to give assistance. Another drawing portrays Ukrainian soldiers forcing Russian soldiers from Ukraine. 'There was a lot of pain, and the children needed to get it out,' says Hanna. 'We can then work with that pain. Our therapist helps the child to grieve.'

The 'after' therapy drawings are dramatically different. Typically the children draw sunrises, mountains, forests, blue skies and houses with well-tended gardens, rich with flowers.

'This is a new period of life for the children,' says Hanna. 'This is about their dreams, thoughts and what life will be like. These are not dark like the before drawings but are about optimism and hope. Some children were not able to draw anything at all at the beginning, so by checking the difference in the drawings that a child does, the therapist is able to chart their progress with expressing their emotions. It's all about giving the children hope that the future can be better than the present.'

There is more than one way to give children hope. While some kids are given a paintbrush to help heal their broken spirits, others are handed cameras.

*

A ten-year-old girl in Chernihiv, in the north of Ukraine,[13] surveys her grandfather's workshop, carefully taking photographs of the sawdust scattered over the floor. To someone walking by, it could look like a child photographing an empty shed, but this girl is documenting the reality of how her life has been devastated by the Russian army.

Masha is using a disposable camera given to her by a 23-year-old student named Artem Skorohodko. When Russia invaded, he asked himself what kind of contribution he could make. His answer was different from many other Ukrainians we met. He asked, 'How could I help to document the war?'

But it wasn't his own perspective he wanted to share, it was that of the children living through the war. Everyone talks about how the war affects children, he tells me, 'but kids are always depicted as a subject, so they never have the opportunity to speak. They are always spoken *of*.' So Artem put his studies on hold to work out how to give these children a voice of their own.

He began travelling to 'deoccupied' areas – parts of Ukraine that had been taken back from the Russians – and giving cameras to children aged from seven to fifteen, but most commonly ten- to twelve-year-olds. 'We teach them how to use the cameras and then we let them go for a few weeks so they can picture everything that they experienced in these villages,' Artem says. The children are guided as to how to record the effect of the war on their friends and family, and at the end of each month, the group gathers to show each other their photos and talk about what impact the war is having on them.

Many of the children found that by doing this they were able to express their feelings in a way they could not if simply asked to talk about the war. 'When we came back with many of the photos printed out,' Artem says, 'they were able to see what they had captured … The stories started flowing and it became for them very much easier to reflect on their experiences.' Often the images seem 'simple and straightforward', but once the children start telling the story about why they took the picture, he says, 'It became evident to me that there was something deeper behind it.'

Artem called the organisation Behind Blue Eyes, an idiom that describes how someone *really* feels, not the strength or blankness they might be projecting to the world. 'Often a person can be deeply traumatised or disturbed on the inside, but you cannot tell it from the outside,' he says. 'They act like regular kids with their fun stuff, throwing a ball, but somewhere deep inside them there is a footprint that the war has left.'

Artem says his project has made him realise that even in war, children understand everything. Even though they might project the air of not caring about what is going on, 'they are super conscious, super talented and they are super aware of their feelings. The only problem is that they cannot express it verbally.'

It's Masha who photographed her grandfather's shed who has made the biggest impression on Artem. Masha's grandfather was a carpenter, and she took a picture of his ruined workshop after the Russians had taken over her town. 'She told me she used to collect sawdust for her hamsters,' he says. 'She had nine or ten hamsters, and when the Russians approached the town, they had to leave them in their house. All of them eventually died because obviously the Russian soldiers didn't look after them. She attributed every one of her stories to these hamsters, and it was a deep loss to her.' She took the photo of the ruined carpentry workshop for one reason: it reminded her of the hamsters. 'You understand how important and significant it was for a kid,' he says.

Another of Masha's photographs is of a backyard sale that Masha organised, in which she sold the things she'd chosen from the humanitarian aid Artem had brought to the village. Her mother bought a cabbage, her grandfather bought a cigarette lighter and her father bought a pair of sneakers because the Russians had taken all his shoes. From the money she raised in the backyard sale Masha bought food for her new hamsters.

Later, with the permission of the children and their parents, Behind Blue Eyes puts on photography exhibitions to raise money. These funds are used to help support the children. Artem often asks the children what they want for their birthday. 'So they write down everything they have been dreaming of.' One thing that surprises Artem is the simplicity of the children's dreams: mobile phones, bicycles, pets. 'One girl asked for a chinchilla,' he remembers, 'and one boy asked for a trip to a waterpark, to go on a water slide.' With the money he raises from the exhibitions, Artem then sees if he can buy the children something they have asked for.

Putting on shows of the photographs has a dual intention. 'What we want to do is preserve the capability of kids to dream and look confidently into the future, regardless of the war trauma they have experienced,' Artem says. 'And second, we want to show kids in these marginalised, remote communities that creativity is something you can build your life upon. It's a serious skill and it enables you to earn money ... We want to challenge the way that creativity is fostered in kids in remote communities. We want to show that creativity is not just for fun, it's not just a set of activities, but it is a state of mind which enables you to earn money and prosper in the modern era.'

Behind Blue Eyes has proved a big success, with children hearing that it is nearby often wanting the team to come to their village so they can join. The reason the program targets liberated areas is that these places have often been the most traumatised by Russian soldiers. Artem says the children swap Vladimir Putin jokes 'like cards', and even though they have seen and felt more than any child their age should have, they have a resilience that Artem thinks some adults lack.

'I am speaking [to] the kids in the front-line villages, the newly liberated regions where you are still constantly hearing the explosions,' he says. 'It is dangerous, but they are still thinking kid stuff, they still act like kids.' The children's ability to persevere despite everything raging about them has brought a certain sense of relief to Artem. 'When the war had started, everything was on a time frame of one week or two weeks,' he says. But ever since he started working with the kids, they empower him to dream about the future, to think where he might be in the next two to five years. 'Doing this work releases me from this box that war essentially puts you in: short-term planning, the sense that I'm screwed, [that] everything is bad, that we'll never come back to the life that we had before.'

Artem is extremely proud of these children. 'This is a huge discovery for me because I think that children are underrated really in terms of how conscious they are, how talented they are, and I would like to be an enabler of this talent – [to] drive it and empower with a new force.' I mention to Artem that from the way he is talking, it seems that the project has taught him a whole culture of giving. 'I am really into giving now,' he says. 'I can watch the children grow, them being happy and contributing to their lives. Even after the war finishes, I want to continue in educational work.'

Thanks to these children, Artem can think beyond next week and into the future to what life will look like after the war. That said, he knows he's not entirely in control of his future. He realises that at some point he may have to give up all this work if he gets a letter calling him up to join the army. 'I'll need to defend my country,' he says. 'I don't feel I have enough confidence to go right now, but if the time comes, if I receive the letter, or if I feel a strong urge to defend and to go, I will do this. I'll go.'

Until then, he'll keep giving these children the best weapon he can: self-expression. But while this story is a positive example of how images can change the way we think and feel about a war, not every photo taken by or of a child is a happy one.

*

As a journalist and former editor of *The Sydney Morning Herald*, I have seen many photographs so confronting that they never made it to publication. This was one of those, a photo I wish I hadn't seen, as the image has been imprinted on my mind.

The photo was of a two-year-old boy in a nappy – a baby, essentially – who'd been in his apartment in Sloviansk one Saturday afternoon when it was hit by a Russian missile. The baby and his father were buried under rubble; his mother had been in a different room and did not take the brunt of the attack. The photo showed the boy being pulled from the rubble by rescuers. What hit me was the boy's rubbery neck, his head flopped to one side. There was no muscle, no strength. The boy looked dead, but he was still alive. Just.

The rescuers rushed him to hospital, but he died a few minutes after that photo was taken. His father was also dead. His mother survived and was taken to hospital. The staff did not tell her that her son and husband were dead. She was in a fragile condition, and they were worried that if they told her the news, she would lose any will to live.

Friends of the family put other photos of the boy on social media. They included one of the boy dressed in a tiny suit for his second birthday, surrounded by balloons. He was beaming with joy, the sort of unbridled happiness typical of a two-year-old who understands that all the fuss of balloons and a cake is for them.

A few minutes after seeing the picture of the barely alive boy, I noticed a story on the Reuters news agency about Vladimir Putin attending a midnight Orthodox Easter service in Moscow that same day. The detail of Putin's Easter service jumped out at me: he was dressed elegantly, wearing a dark blue suit with a purple tie. He blessed himself eight times, Reuters reported.

Here was a man at the height of his power, wearing an expensive suit and with the luxury of being able to bless himself. Eight times. And here was a baby in nappies – powerless, with minutes to live, a broken neck. On the same Easter Sunday that Putin was blessing himself, the Russian army fired S-300 missiles and destroyed the Ukrainian Orthodox Church of St Michael the Archangel near Zaporizhzhia in southeastern Ukraine.

Ukrainians were seeing these sorts of photos every day. They were hearing these stories constantly, not as news items on their phones but as real stories about their neighbours, families and friends. When I realised this, it helped me to understand the absolute rage that many Ukrainians felt every day and their determination to defeat Russia. This anger explained why an entire country united behind Zelensky's call to arms.

I would often think about the photo of the boy as I travelled around Ukraine. The first time I saw it, I remember thinking that this was a morally unambiguous war. Of course there were two sides, as there is to every story, but certain facts were clear. Russia is the aggressor. Russia invaded Ukraine. Russia continues to launch attacks. Ukraine is the victim.

When it came to Vladimir Putin versus this nameless boy, this was not a fair fight.

That boy in the nappy never stood a chance.

CHAPTER 6

Cyber fighters

Illia Vitiuk wants to see Vladimir Putin dead. I meet him in the Stalinist-style Ukrainian intelligence headquarters in Kyiv, a building once used by the Soviet Union as the headquarters of the KGB in Ukraine. Apart from Moscow, this was the KGB's biggest branch office, as Ukraine was one of the most important of the former Soviet Union countries. I mention to Vitiuk that there's a good chance that Putin, a long-time KGB officer, would have spent time in this very building. Vitiuk looks at me with an expression that is part anger and part death stare: 'Putin won't be here again. Only in a casket.'

This building houses the country's main and most secretive intelligence agency, the Security Service of Ukraine (SBU). The agency is different from any Australian model. In Australia and the UK, the Australian Security Intelligence Organisation (ASIO) and MI5 focus on domestic security, the Australian Secret Intelligence Service (ASIS) and MI6 focus on recruiting agents who live overseas, and the Australian Federal Police (AFP) and UK National Crime Agency focus on national law enforcement. The SBU does all three – it's heavily involved in domestic security, monitors overseas threats to Ukraine and engages in special operations on its own soil if it needs to, such as during a hostage crisis or terrorist attack. The SBU is therefore both an intelligence-gathering and law enforcement agency.

To even get into this building in central Kyiv is a high-level security experience. Parking is not possible outside, and soldiers guard the perimeter and monitor approaching pedestrians. As I walk through this Soviet nostalgia with its dour staircases and corridors, I pass members of the elite Alpha unit, identifiable through their distinctive fatigue markings. This is one of Ukraine's top echelons of special forces who conduct the most complicated and dangerous missions. Even within the SBU – itself an elite agency – the Alpha forces have a revered status as the unit that can do missions other units find too difficult or dangerous, such as dealing with terrorist attacks or rescuing hostages. On the walls are dramatic pictures of Alpha teams in action, arming self-detonating drones with explosives, operating anti-tank missiles and storming buildings with dogs. In these photos the identities of the Alpha teams are concealed.

My meeting today is with Illia Vitiuk, the head of the SBU's cyber intelligence team. In the world's first full cyber war, Vitiuk is one of Ukraine's stormtroopers. He runs a department responsible for strategic threats to cyber security. 'We deal with counterintelligence, counterterrorism and organised crime that can threaten the state security of the country,' he explains.

The chief function of the unit is to learn about any individuals or organisations – either in Russia or Ukraine – who are working to try to damage Ukraine's cyber security. He lists some of the tasks under his purview: deflecting cyber attacks, defence of critical IT infrastructure, information security, countering disinformation campaigns and special psychological operations. 'We are not just countering cyber attacks,' he says, 'but we also investigate crimes, cyber espionage and cyber terrorism conducted by our enemy today.'

The attacks on Ukraine did not just begin with the 2022 invasion. Vitiuk says Russia's 'cyber aggression' began in 2014 when it invaded Crimea. Since then, the number of cyber attacks has constantly grown from year to year. In 2020, the SBU recorded 800 cyber attacks on critical infrastructure. In 2021, they recorded 1400, and in 2022 it was 4500. 'Today we know how to cope with it because we have a great experience since 2014,' he says.

Before the war, both Russia and Ukraine were two of the world's cyber giants, their criminals employing the latest technologies. They sometimes even worked together, with many cyber gangs having both Russian and Ukrainian members housed and protected in both countries. 'Nobody knows Russian capabilities better than us,' Vitiuk says. While they used to team up to take down common enemies, all that has changed – now they are turning their cyber capabilities on each other.

Those cyber guns are sometimes combined with real ones. Vitiuk says Russia often combines cyber attacks with what are called 'kinetic' attacks, the military term for physical warfare. He says it's not uncommon that at the same time the Russian army is trying to physically destroy something such as a power plant, a cyber team will be trying to hack into their computer systems to make defence of the facility more difficult. Or Russia will launch a cyber attack on an energy facility to cause chaos before it makes a physical attack with a missile or drone. 'They don't care about people, they don't care about their lives, they don't care about children,' he says. 'They will switch off the electricity in hospitals without even thinking about it.'

Vitiuk believes that this is the first fully co-ordinated cyber and physical war. So while many other countries are helping Ukraine by assisting with military support, when I meet Vitiuk he is also asking for cyber support. 'Due to the immense growth in the number of cyber attacks and cyber aggression, we need additional software and additional hardware,' he says. 'We need different forensic equipment. We need experts and expertise that will help us to multiply our offensive and defensive capabilities.'

Vitiuk's argument for allies to support Ukraine's cyber defence echoes that of President Zelensky for supporting Ukraine's military effort: if Russia defeats Ukraine, then other countries will be at risk from Russia. He says that Ukraine is keeping Russia 'busy' in the cyber world, which means Moscow has less time and fewer resources to focus on countries such as Australia.

'Russia can target Australia and all other countries supporting Ukraine,' he says. 'But what is important to understand is that Ukraine is a very big country. We have a lot of IT infrastructure they are trying to attack, and we are pretty successful in defending ourselves and countering these attacks. That means that our work makes them busy.' Vitiuk describes Ukraine as 'a shield to the whole world'. 'And that's why I always say that our partners should be interested in helping us. And by helping us, they are actually helping themselves,' he says.

Ukraine is getting a crash course in Russia's most current cyber attack techniques; they know the enemy and are prepared to distribute what they're learning with their allies. 'We are ready to share this knowledge and this experience with the world,' Vitiuk says. 'It's very important to understand that there's no country in the world that should feel safe with today's Russia, with insane leaders that are there today. But unfortunately, we have to understand that probably Russia is not the last powerful country with leaders that can threaten the world.' Lessons learnt in the Ukraine war won't just be applicable to Ukraine and Russia but the whole world, he says. 'I do believe that this experience will be useful for any country.'

But while it's noble to think about the lessons that will be shared at the end of this war, the reality is that Vitiuk and the rest of Ukraine is now deeply immersed in it, and clearly they're in it for the long haul. 'We will do our best and we will fight as long as it will be needed. And we are ready to pay the ultimate price for our freedom,' he says. 'Our president showed this, and our regular people somewhere in trenches also showed that they will pay, they will give their lives in order to keep our country free and independent.'

President Zelensky's decision to remain in Ukraine after Russia invaded rather than flee the country and run the war from Poland inspired many Ukrainians. 'I cannot even describe how important it was,' Vitiuk says. 'Our president is a hero, and the understanding of it gives us power to continue to be more courageous, more brave, and ready to pay the ultimate price because he showed us that he's ready by staying here in Kyiv … He showed us how to react and what to do. And many people who were not knowing what to do, whether to run or to stay, they saw the President being here and they were absolutely decisive in a way what they are about to do next. So his role during the first day and then, after that, his bravery, his strong position, his work twenty-four seven, what he actually did. I saw him not sleeping for a very long time because he had so much to do in the very beginning to ignite the whole world to help Ukraine.'

The same cannot be said about Putin, sitting in his palaces in Russia. In my travels over four decades, I've found that most people attempt to be diplomatic about their enemies, initially at least. But in Ukraine, people across the board – both leaders and ordinary people – did not even attempt any qualifications when talking about Vladimir Putin. Vitiuk is typical when I ask him what Ukrainians think of Putin. 'They hate him,' he says. 'He has brought so much blood, so much horror and grief to our country.' Vitiuk adds that this hatred goes beyond Putin and onto the whole Russian people, regardless of whether they are strongly supporting him or simply neutral. 'They're not doing anything to stop this war. And we do believe that these people are also responsible, and they will also have to pay the price for that.'

I ask Vitiuk what price these people would pay. He gave the example of what happened in Germany after World War II, when the country had to constantly teach their children the lesson of what they had done to make sure it would not happen again. 'So probably something like this should happen to all

Russians, no matter whether they were military,' he says. 'If they were military and they were responsible for some crimes, they will be brought to court. If they are just regular people, they will suffer some … kind of re-education to understand that this was horrible and this should never happen again.'

Vitiuk had an interesting point of view on how this war could end. Instead of one side or the other winning militarily, he thought that the end of the existence of Russia in its current form was the only way. 'There should be some kind of revolution,' he suggests. 'Some democratic powers should come and redesign the whole policy of Russia and the whole understanding of Russia's role in the world.' However, he does not know how long that will take. He gives the historical example of how the USSR slowly disintegrated over forty-five years, from the end of World War II until the collapse of the empire in 1991. Vitiuk doesn't think it'll take another ten years for the current iteration of Russia to crumble. 'Now the world is much faster due to information technologies. I do believe that it won't take as long time,' he says. And he thinks the rest of the world is on his side. 'We do see that this willingness and understanding of all the democratic world, that Russia in the way it exists now should stop existing, is clear and obvious.'

Whenever this war is over, Vitiuk is hopeful for Ukraine's future. 'I do believe that for Ukraine after the war, a great future is on the way because we will rebuild everything here. We will change our philosophy. We will move even further from the Soviet ideology and understanding of things. And I do believe that the result of this war will be a strong impulse for our development.' From Vitiuk's perspective, this is especially true when it comes to Ukraine's standing in technology, which will 'help us to build strong capabilities for leadership in cyber in the world after this war'.

Through surviving Russia's virtual onslaught year after year, Vitiuk's team at the SBU are one of the toughest and most resilient cyber intelligence operations you'll find anywhere. And when you pair them with their colleagues I'm about to meet at another cyber unit in Ukraine, it makes them a formidable force.

*

Across town in a large building on the outskirts of Kyiv, I've just walked into Ukraine's cyber-security control room. The moment you enter this establishment, you can sense the intensity. This is the headquarters of the National Cyber Security Co-ordination Centre (NCSCC), one of the key parts of Ukraine's cyber operation that reports directly to President Zelensky. The centre was established in 2016, two years after Russia's invasion of Crimea, as a response to Russia's increased cyber attacks against Ukraine. In its headquarters, thirty senior analysts are fixated on their computers, trying to spot cyber attacks as quickly as possible after they've been launched.

These teams are monitoring Russian cyber attacks on Ukrainian infrastructure in real time. The first room I enter is a large open-plan office with teams of people monitoring their screens. They're scouring through Ukrainian sites and computer networks trying to find evidence of unusual activity. Sometimes a hacker can 'sit' inside a target network for weeks or months, observing activity and harvesting information. The NCSCC's role is to spot this infiltration then expunge the hacker from the network. The people in this centre are trying to find vulnerabilities in both Ukrainian and Russian networks – if they find those vulnerabilities in Ukrainian networks, they put in place defensive software. If they find them in Russian networks, they pass this information on to special teams who will then try to hack into the system and wreak havoc on the Russians.

I'm taken into the most sensitive room of all, a control room with a huge screen that takes up an entire wall. A team of six people sit staring at it. The screen carries a running sheet of various 'bad actors', cyber gangs known to the Ukrainians because they are repeat hacking offenders. Most are from Russia, but some are from Iran and North Korea. Each of the gangs uses particular types of virtual viruses to infiltrate computer networks, and the moment this centre detects evidence of one of those viruses, it flashes a warning about which branch of the government or military or intelligence network the looming hack is occurring in and which gang appears to be behind it. Those in the room then try to block the virus.

While the SBU is seeking intelligence to crush hacking networks, the NCSCC's role is to intercept possible cyber attacks in real time, particularly in their early stages. Sometimes the NCSCC can spot an imminent cyber attack by unusual behaviour then seek to protect the targeted Ukrainian network. The NCSCC also has teams trained to discover when a 'malevolent actor' – also known as a hacker – has actually infiltrated a network.

The head of operations here, Serhii Prokopenko, tells me that the importance of the team's work is shown by the fact that he and the NCSCC report directly to President Zelensky. As I stand with Prokopenko looking at the large board showing which gangs are currently attacking Ukraine, he points out that the majority are from Russia, with one or two from North Korea, such as the Lazarus Group.

One of those on Ukraine's 'top ten' list of attackers is REvil (short for Ransomware Evil), a Russian-based gang notorious for ransomware attacks: hacking into a computer system and demanding a ransom to leave without destroying it. On one trip to Ukraine I investigated, with a *Four Corners*[14] team, REvil and found the gang has been strongly linked to Russia's intelligence service, the FSB. Before the invasion of Ukraine, under pressure from the US where major companies had been hacked by REvil, Russia raided the group and jailed some of its leaders. But after the invasion, the FSB released the leaders it had imprisoned and – crucially – asked them to work for the state. Putin engineered for them to pivot from criminal activity seeking ransoms from major companies to joining the war effort and attempting to crash Ukraine's cyber systems.

We're not immune either. In 2022, REvil – or at least a gang using its software – attempted to break into one of Australia's largest health insurers, Medibank, which affected 9.7 million current and former customers. In that cyber attack, to increase the pressure on Medibank to pay a ransom, the hackers released a list of customers' private details on the internet. Under the headline 'Naughty List', they posted the personal information of people who had had pregnancy terminations or treatment for drug addictions and mental illnesses. On the advice of the Australian government, Medibank refused to pay. In an unusual move for the Australian media – which is famously divided into factions – all publications unanimously agreed that no publicity would be given to any of the intimate medical details used to try to blackmail Medibank into paying a ransom, and it was this agreement by the media that rendered the blackmail threat meaningless. In my assessment, the response to the Medibank hack was a gold standard for how the media should work together to remove the power of cyber blackmailers. The media removed the only leverage that the blackmailers had: fear that people's intimate medical details would be exposed.

What happens here in Ukraine therefore impacts the future of cyberattacks in Australia. I'm visiting this cyber security centre in Kyiv with two former Australian army officers, David Robinson and Robert Potter, who are helping the Ukrainians to shore up their defences against Russian cyber attacks. As we're talking, the power in the centre cuts, not an uncommon occurrence in wartime Ukraine. But standing in darkness doesn't stop Serhii Prokopenko from answering my questions. I ask him if there's likely to be an increase in the number of attacks by Russian cyber gangs on Australia in retaliation for the support we have given to Ukraine. 'Yes,' he answers without hesitation. 'Russia is finding it harder to get success here so will target Australia and other countries who have supported Ukraine.'

*

A strong Ukraine is therefore a strong Australia, and these two Australian cyber experts have been embraced by Ukraine's intelligence services to assist in their war effort. David Robinson and Robert Potter have been spending months in Kyiv helping key Ukrainian agencies fortify themselves against cyber attacks.

They invite me to the Kyiv office opening of their company, Internet 2.0. Addressing the crowd, Potter says, 'About six months ago we made a decision that we would come to Ukraine. Not just simply because of how impressed we were with how the people of Ukraine had responded to the war and showed the world what it could do but because we also had a theory about cyber security as a concept: that unlike most other fields, this is not gardening, this is not bricklaying, this is an industry with an enemy and an industry with an ideology. This is where the enemy is trying to get to. And this is where our new allies are.'

Yegor Dubinsky, the deputy minister for digital transformation in charge of cyber security, is one of the speakers at the launch. He tells me that despite Russia being aggressive, their cyber attacks have not been as effective as Ukraine anticipated. 'After the invasion we had a massive amount [of cyber attacks], but we had an eight-year preparation,' he says, referring to the fact that most Ukrainians believe the war with Russia began in 2014 when Russia invaded Crimea.

Potter agrees. 'Luckily the Russians gave them nearly a decade's notice to prepare for conflict, and the Ukrainians used that time well and generated a really powerful military that has surprised the world.'

Even though Internet 2.0 is an Australian-based company, they made the decision to move their operations to Ukraine and were the first cyber-security company in the world to do so. 'A lot of companies are trying to work in Ukraine, but they're trying to do it from elsewhere,' Potter explains. 'Some companies have left Ukraine to try to reduce their risk threshold, but we think it's incredibly important for us to be here, and we think that by coming here we'll show people that you can actually run a normal business in spite of the situation, especially if you have something really meaningful to do.'

When talking about Ukraine and its war effort, Potter refers to 'the enemy'. I ask if Russia is an enemy of both Ukraine and Australia. 'When you're in cyber security, you have to be comfortable with the reality that there is a bad guy out there,' says Potter. 'It's a mentality shift. Not all cyber companies understand that. You have to be willing to talk about the fact that there is an enemy out there that is trying to hurt your networks. The same hackers that are trying to take Ukraine out of the war are the same hackers that took a bunch of private information from Australian citizens at Medibank.'

Either Russia's cyber gang REvil or another gang using its software was responsible for the Medibank hack in Australia in 2022. Another malware operation similar to REvil is Conti, a RaaS (ransomware as a service) model used to infiltrate targets. I asked Potter how he knows these operations are being propped up by Russia. 'These gangs have professed their explicit affinity and loyalty to the Russian government and the Russian cause,' he says. 'Conti, for example, made a public statement saying that it was working on behalf of the Russian state … It's not subtle, it's not secret, and they're very, very closely aligned with the Russian government.'

Over several days with Potter in Kyiv visiting places such as the SBU, I remark that it's clear how passionate he is about Ukraine. 'I am passionate because Ukraine is a democracy, and because I'm tired of watching the faces of victims of cyber attacks,' he says. 'I've spent my career as an incident responder. I've responded to some of the largest cyber attacks that have been undertaken in Australia. I've watched the North Korean government raid Third World banks for money to pay for a nuclear program. I've seen some of the worst behaviour in the digital space and I've worked with the victims of these attacks for more than a decade. I'm passionate because I don't believe it's a reality that we have to live with. I believe we can fight back against this criminal enterprise.'

The day after the launch of Potter and Robinson's company, I enter a makeshift cyber headquarters in a Kyiv hotel. I'm impressed by what I see. Several monitors have been set up around a number of computers in what amounts to a pop-up cyber-security headquarters, room service included. I'm sitting with David Robinson and Rafiq Jabrayilov, one of his security engineers who's flown in from Canberra. What I'm witnessing on the screens is fascinating: in real time, we're watching Russian hacking attempts.

Robinson and Jabrayilov have a vast network of servers around the world, from 'honeypots' designed to lure and therefore reveal possible hackers, to servers of their own clients and their own networks. The screens in front of us are monitoring for alerts that are indicators of ongoing cyber attacks. They're looking for 'cyber events', which are abnormal activities, so they can try to track the IP addresses of whomever is causing them. They're also looking for 'IOCs' – indicators of compromise. This is monitored data that matches against a preprogrammed list of known threats, setting off an alarm if they're discovered. In summary, if unusual activity matches with the long list of software from hackers, the alarms will go off. This team can then alert the client, whether it's a private client in Australia or one of the Ukrainian defence agencies.

'What we're trying to do here is to help protect Ukrainian computer networks such as critical infrastructure and power networks, hospitals, key facilities that are vulnerable to cyber attack,' Robinson says. He explains that their goal in Ukraine is to set up a technology known as a 'cloaking firewall'. It's a disruptive defensive cyber technology that the Ukrainians want to deploy throughout their critical infrastructure and wider cyber-security posture. 'What the cloaking firewall is doing is transiting all that data through computer systems that can be flagged for threats,' he explains. 'If the Russians, for example, were hacking one of the computer networks that we're protecting, we can use algorithms to flag and view that threat, and then we can basically block it.'

While Internet 2.0 has set up in Kyiv to help defend Ukrainian infrastructure, Robinson says that he's also got something to learn while he's here. 'We're also here to learn from the Ukrainians about Russian cyber activity,' Robinson says. 'They're at the front of the entire cyber war, and so we can learn a lot from Ukraine as well.'

As I sit with Jabrayilov looking at these monitors, I remark that it seems an extraordinary situation that here is someone from a quiet suburb of Canberra sitting in a hotel room in Kyiv at the forefront of a cyber war between Russia and Ukraine. 'It feels great,' he says. 'It's a big pleasure for me to help Ukraine in these hard times, to help Ukraine protect itself from the Russian invaders.'

I suggest to him that there's probably somebody sitting in Russia trying to counter the various measures that he's putting in place. 'Yes, I believe people in Russia are always trying to work out how to get around these types of securities, to break them. But we keep improving ours. As much as they are developing their skills to break the system, we are always developing our systems to make sure we are ahead of them.' So it's a non-stop battle? 'Cyber war between engineers and attackers is never-ending,' Jabrayilov says. 'As much as they are improving their skills, we need to do it twice or three times faster to be ahead of them. So far, we're winning.'

That doesn't mean there aren't close calls. When tracking attempted Russian cyber attacks, Robinson says there's sometimes an 'OF [Oh fuck!] moment' He describes one of these for me: 'If you see something you don't normally see, you see a lot of alerts,' he says. 'But if you see that red alert that you know is a serious malware alert, there's a lot of swearing going on at the computer.'

Jabrayilov says that while they haven't had any disasters, Russians do attack their systems. In fact, they can see the attackers' IP addresses on their dashboards when they're doing it. So while this side of the war takes place on computers, it can still feel very personal. 'We can see exact locations – where they are attacking from,' he says. 'If we go deep we can get more information, but we think that's unnecessary and we don't have the time and resources to track them down … Our purpose is to protect, not to track them down.'

As the three of us sit watching this seemingly buzzing cyber war between Russia and Ukraine play out on the monitors, Robinson makes an observation on the future of these technologies: 'Cyber security is the new space race.'

*

While spending time in Kyiv gave me an up-close micro view of the cyber war, I'm keen to get the macro view. Back in Australia, a *Four Corners* team I'm working with asks around the cyber community for who is regarded as one of the smartest analysts. Many people point us towards Katherine Mansted, someone who has closely watched the Ukraine war playing out in the cyber world. She is executive director of cyber intelligence at CyberCX, a cutting-edge Australian cyber-security company.

In particular, Mansted has studied how Russia has tried to co-ordinate cyber attacks with conventional military operations. She says Russia had more success at the beginning of the war. 'It did better perhaps because it had more time to plan and co-ordinate,' she says. 'Back in the first week of the war, we saw a really deliberate attempt by Russia to combine the conventional, the cyber and also the informational dimension of its conflict. For Russia at first, controlling communications and telecommunications was key to its strategy.' She describes how in the first week, there was a missile strike on a broadcasting tower as well as a cyber attack on a broadcasting company and a broader misinformation campaign.

Mansted says it's important to look at the war in the context of Russia's declaration that it was going to disable the 'disinformation system' of Ukraine. It targeted people on social media and the elderly via phone calls with the aim of creating chaos. 'It was about sapping the morale and the will of the people of Ukraine to fight back against invasion,' she says, 'and it was a pretty good example of Russia both pursuing a conventional strategy and a cyber strategy ... to control that broadcasting sphere, to control communications and to effect a sense of chaos, really, among the people it was trying to invade.'

Whether it's taking place on the ground or behind a computer screen, it's all the same war, says Mansted. 'We fight wars in land, air, sea, space, cyber – they're all connected.' But one surprise has been Russia not having the level of co-ordination that many expected them to. 'We thought they were probably going to be a little bit better and more successful than they have been,' Mansted says. 'A lot of Russian criminal actions or activist actions that have been claimed to have been supporting Russia have not been that effective. They've more been mildly disruptive.' She describes how they're defacing websites, temporarily disrupting operations and sometimes even claiming hacks that might not even be theirs. 'So there's also a dimension that criminals are looking for a PR opportunity here as well,' she says. 'They're claiming and perhaps overstating their attacks.'

Mansted says the motivation for using a cyber or kinetic attack to wreak havoc changes over time. Before the invasion of Ukraine, Russia was favouring clandestine virtual attacks that were harder to trace. But now that the two countries are openly at war, it's not afraid to literally bring out the heavy arsenal. 'When Russia turned the lights out for many Ukrainians back in 2015,' she says, 'it used cyber to do that because it was deniable, because it was covert, because they could frustrate attribution. Of course, now we're in open hostilities, most of the energy terrorism, to use President Zelensky's words, that Russia has been waging against Ukraine is with missiles and drones. Because when the gloves are off, you can use those kinetic weapons that maybe you wouldn't use during peacetime.'

The Ukrainians have assembled some pretty impressive cyber defences, according to Mansted. And the rest of the world is watching them. What are the implications of the cyber war in Ukraine for the next major war? Mansted says every cyber defender and attacker around the world will be looking at the war and learning lessons from Russia's successes and failures – particularly on the failure front. 'In the next war I would expect we'll see adaptation and an even closer interlinkage between [cyber and kinetic] domains,' she says. 'I would anticipate we'll see even more planning, more prepositioning so that critical infrastructure is held at risk from day one or day zero of a conflict, if not before.'

So has the face of war been changed forever? 'I think the face of war was changing already,' Mansted says. 'Conflict has been changing for a decade or more. Russia and Ukraine have been at cyber war for a decade. There are other instances of some pretty aggressive cyber activity during peacetime around the world. What we've seen here is those two things colliding: cyber conflict and a real-world kinetic conflict. As war returns to the European continent in a pretty visceral way, they're combining.'

The Ukraine war has shown the power that civilian entities can bring to cyber defence. 'Ukraine has showcased beautifully that we can have industry, private sector and ordinary citizens working together,' Mansted says. 'Cyber defence is a team sport in Ukraine.'

The backbone of Ukraine's volunteer army has been the younger generation, and this is especially true when it comes to all things online. Take Daryna Antoniuk, a 21-year-old technology journalist. Her friends have joined what she calls 'the IT army', using their spare time to try to hack Russians and create chaos within the enemy. 'The war is a full-time job,' she says. 'I became stronger, resilient, and can work under stress. Writing a story during a missile strike or reporting from a place where people have died changes you. It's hard to perceive the world as you did before.'

Similarly to Daryna, many Ukrainians told me that they now have both a day and a night job. By day they do their regular work, but come five or six in the afternoon they switch to their night job, which is often a technology-related way to support the war effort. Some try to hack into the computer networks of various Russian agencies, and as you're about to learn, some are using their technological skills in one of the biggest growth areas of our time: drone warfare.

CHAPTER 7

The drone busters

I'LL NEVER FORGET THE SOUND. IT IS ABOUT 3 AM AND Sylvie and I wake to a strange noise outside our Kyiv hotel room, like a whipper-snipper for trimming lawns. We go to the balcony and above us see the unmistakeable flying stingray silhouette of a drone. It is an extraordinary moment to know that thirty or forty metres from us is a triangular death machine that could drop its package of explosives wherever it wants and is probably being controlled by someone on a computer in Russia or Belarus. For good reasons, Ukrainians call these drones 'birds of death'.

We record the eerie sound of the Iranian-made Shahid drone. Even though we know being this close is not safe, it is flying away from us towards the city centre, so we feel the danger is reduced. We are not its intended target.

To shoot down a drone, the Ukrainians work out which way the drone is flying and then fire hundreds of bullets into the air from mobile rapid response vehicles, creating a 'wall'. The drone is almost certain to fly into one of them, and that creates a massive bang as the explosives detonate. In all our time in Ukraine, we never got used to waking in the middle of the night to the dramatic sound of explosions.

About thirty seconds after the drone flies past our balcony, Ukraine's aerial-defence team unleashes a barrage of bullets towards it, destroying the drone about a kilometre from us. All of this lights up the sky. One more of Russia's birds of death shot down.

Just as this is the first war between two cyber giants, it's also the first full drone war. This is not just military versus military, and cyber versus cyber, but drone versus drone.

Cyber technology and drones are now built into the military strategies of both Russia and Ukraine. Both sides use battalions of drones to hit the other, and in Ukraine there are an estimated eighty drone factories in Kyiv alone. But while these drone factories have quickly sprung up in Ukraine, the same did not happen in Russia. Instead, they spent the first year relying on Shahid drones bought from Iran. After a year the Russians began producing their own on an industrial scale as they turned warehouses and some supermarkets into drone factories. But the Ukrainians have been working on their own supplies for some time as well as making great leaps in drone technology. Due to the pressures of war, Ukrainians quickly came to be regarded as the world's best when it came to drones. In basements and town halls across the country, thousands of Ukrainians are making drones as part of the countrywide fightback against Russia.

*

It's Friday night in Kyiv and Sylvie and I are waiting for an Uber with an old rocker who has a new mission in life: making drones. We met Oleksandr Pipa, one of Ukraine's original punk rockers, earlier in this book when he told us how he'd watched the initial Russian incursion from his window before rushing to help set up checkpoints and medical tents in his suburb for soldiers being brought back from the rapidly shifting front lines.

Now he's found a new role in life, as each evening, he and fellow musician Anton Chernysh get together to make drones. Sylvie and I tag along as they head to a secret location in Kyiv. 'Drones are very expensive,' Oleksandr says. 'That is why we have started designing our own version of the drones that we use for surveillance and also to deliver some "presents",' he says with a grin. Many Ukrainians involved in making drones call the explosives they attach 'presents' or 'gifts' for Russian soldiers.

Once there, we go to the basement where the two musicians have set up an extraordinary drone factory complete with

3D-printing machines provided by a Ukrainian company, models of various drones and anti-drone guns.

'This basement is our main research laboratory,' Anton says. 'All the groups where we have fighters, volunteers and so on are doing almost the same thing as us, but this lab is the heart of inventions, which we later share with others.'

Anton, twenty-seven, whose photo appears on the cover of this book, is a mild-mannered IT consultant and musician. He's using the technology smarts he developed in his career to help the war effort. In this basement factory, he shows us the workstations he's built for anyone who wants to help, like Oleksandr, who comes along for several hours each evening. Anton had expertise in IT before the war while Oleksandr has simply learnt on the job under Anton's guidance.

We mention to them that it's a Friday night, and before the war began, musicians like themselves might be performing. 'I would normally be playing in a pub or drinking some beer, but now I cannot afford having fun,' Anton says. 'It's a war, and I'm fighting for our survival … Every single Ukrainian is fighting for survival. But we often also have something personal.' He tells us that his parents' home was invaded in the first hours of the war. About five hundred Russian military vehicles stopped in their village and fought their neighbours for one and a half months. 'It went from being a peaceful village in Ukraine to one occupied by Russian soldiers,' he says.

He quit his job that day. 'I could not sit in front of a computer attending long calls and meetings with customers because I knew what was going on outside,' he says. He began transporting elderly people from Kyiv towards western Ukraine, and because he had a permit to leave the country, he began going to Poland to buy supplies for the army. He would purchase things like body armour in Poland, deliver them to Lviv, and then other volunteers took them to Kyiv.

He tells us about an old lady that one of his volunteers met while making deliveries to a village the Russians had recently left, who was crying and wanting to kiss the feet of the volunteers. 'She told the story of how fourteen Russians came to her apartment, killed her husband and threw him from the window. Then they raped the granddaughter and did the same to the daughter, and they made her watch this,' Anton says. 'That is why she was saying, "Give me some weapons, give me something, I have nothing to live for now and I want to join you."'

Anton says that when Russia decided to invade Ukraine, it did not factor in Ukraine's army of civilians. 'At the beginning it was [the Russian army's] role to come to Kyiv, to kill Zelensky and be done,' he says. 'But there was a huge misunderstanding from their side. They are not fighting against the Ukrainian army, the Ukrainian president or the Ukrainian parliament – they are fighting against the whole population of Ukraine.'

Anton wanted to work out what he could contribute to the volunteer army and how he could be involved. Instead of using his body, though, he realised he could use his mind. 'I started making drones and the release mechanisms for them and collecting requests from the army at the front,' he says. 'I started providing whatever I could to help them from a technical perspective.'

This basement has been fitted with a wall of 3D printers producing parts for drones and for the mechanisms that Anton has designed, which are attached to the drones and release the bombs. Some of these drones are for reconnaissance while others carry what Anton calls 'the candies' – explosives – that the Ukrainian army drops on Russian positions. Working alongside Anton in this basement, punk rocker Oleksandr says he's watched footage of Russian soldiers reacting when they see the drones. 'They hear this noise, they start to panic, it's like a chaos,' he says. 'They try to hide. They don't know what explosives it may have. Sometimes they are regular surveillance drones but sometimes they carry something.'

Anton proudly shows us various drones. We ask how he feels about preparing machines designed to kill people. 'At the very beginning, I had bad feelings,' he says. 'I felt sorry for those guys, but after a while I found myself no longer feeling any regret.' This desensitisation was something we encountered a lot. 'It's a rule of war: they are not people, they are invaders,' he says.

'Either we eliminate them or they kill us. It's that simple: kill or be killed.'

We ask him what Russian soldiers would think if they saw one of these drones approaching. 'If you're a Russian soldier and you see it coming,' he says, 'it is the last thing you see coming.'

Anton and Oleksandr receive requests from the front line as to which types of drones are needed – reconnaissance, medical or attack – and then go through the orders, building whatever is requested. Tonight the two are unpacking parts, welding and wiring all kinds of drones. The range is extraordinary. In one corner are 'kamikaze' drones: the explosives go on the bottom and there are triggers to fire up the detonator. They're called kamikaze drones as they'll also blow up with their packages. Once Anton and Oleksandr make these drones, they hand them over to soldiers who attach the explosives.

On another bench are surveillance drones originally made for film and television production, but their excellent cameras and zooms have made them desirable for the war effort. They also have altitude and obstacle sensors, which allows Ukrainian soldiers to use these drones to see the position and movements of Russian soldiers; at night, the sensors can also pick up the heat of a Russian body.

On yet another bench is a do-it-yourself kit drone. The two musicians use fundraised money to buy all the components from China or from inside Ukraine, and one of these little DIY drones can carry up to two kilograms and fly two kilometres. They may look like toys, but Anton says if a tank is hit in the right spot – particularly if the drone is flown into the tank while the turret is open – they can destroy it.

In another corner of this basement is a Russian reconnaissance drone that Anton souvenired from the front line when Russians soldiers fled. He studies this drone with great interest; he and other Ukrainians I met making drones always valued the chance to study the enemy's weapons up close.

Drones are important in this war, Anton says, because they save lives. 'When we have a drone, we do not have to put people to find out what is out there,' he says, 'and it is better for us to lose the drone than it is to lose a human in the war.'

Oleksandr echoes this view. 'We can sacrifice the drones, [but] our soldiers' lives are important, and that is why the more drones we have, the more human lives will be saved.'

It can also give someone the chance to surrender. In this war of drones, there is now a protocol understood by both sides. If a Ukrainian drone comes across a group of Russian soldiers, it will try to fire at them or drop explosives. But if it comes across a solitary Russian soldier, it will try to capture him instead. 'Drones can be used to show the enemy to surrender,' Anton explains. 'If [Russian soldiers] see a drone that goes like this' – he wiggles his flat palm from side to side – 'it means, "Surrender – immediately drop your weapon, lift up your hands and follow the drone." The drone will take them to a safe place where they will be picked up by a Ukrainian soldier, and you will be still alive and stay alive.' If the soldier tries instead to shoot down the drone or to run away, the drone will fire.

What's going on in this basement is not the reality that either musician imagined for himself a couple of years ago. But making drones makes Oleksandr feel like he's involved. 'It feels important that we are contributing to winning this war,' he says. 'It's Friday night, and usually us musicians should be performing or rehearsing, having fun, but we are making these devices because we hate war.' He's someone who likes to joke and have a laugh, he says, 'but when there is a war, I can't do that: I have to be serious, and I hate that. We need to push out these invaders from our country and [see] their empire collapse, and then we can get back to our normal life – to playing gigs.'

Up until now, Oleksandr has been a lifelong pacifist. As he sits working on a drone, he tells us a story from his childhood. 'The last time I went fishing – it was in fact the first *and* last time I went fishing! – I was six years old,' he begins. 'I caught the fish, but I felt sorry for the fish and I let it go.' He says that he hates hunting; he doesn't like people killing animals just for fun. 'I am a very peaceful person, but what I am doing now is producing devices that will kill the invaders,' he continues, 'and I feel quite good about that because they are invaders. They came here to kill us, so it is either them or us.

'When we're talking about killing Russian soldiers, I would not use the word "killing",' he argues. 'The military terminology is more appropriate. The military never use the word "killing" but rather use "eliminate",' because when it comes to the military, it is a hard job, and you don't think about them as a human beings. You have to destroy them, and that's it.'

Oleksandr realised before this invasion that his view of Russians and the friendships he'd built over years of performing were deteriorating. 'I had my mind changed before the war. I thought I had a lot of good friends, musicians, we used to perform together,' he says. 'I thought they felt the same as I do about the collapse of the Soviet Union, but gradually I saw them change. Once Russia became richer, with oil prices going higher, they were coming back to this natural state, this state of feeling superior.'

We heard many variations of this sentiment when travelling around Ukraine, that while Ukrainians and Russians had for some time thought of themselves as colleagues or even friends of sorts, the power dynamic between the two countries had shifted more and more dramatically in the lead-up to the war and overshadowed many relationships. According to Oleksandr, that's not a coincidence. 'Millions of Ukrainians have finally had their eyes opened,' he says. 'Russians invested billions in their cultural expansions about brainwashing, how Russia is attractive, and how a lot of people want to live in Russia. They claimed a lot of Ukrainians had felt that way, and how a lot of Russian politicians were performing quite well here. They had a lot of supporters here. Now it's over.'

Anton was one of those people who had been made to feel lesser by the Russian propaganda, which extended not just throughout Ukraine but worldwide. He says that when travelling before the invasion and people asked him where he was from, he would say, 'I am from Ukraine,' and they would reply, 'Is that the same as Russia?' He says he doesn't get asked that anymore. 'I feel much more proud than before. I was, to be honest, even trying to hide the fact that I was from Ukraine, because it used to be considered as a bad country ... But now I am so proud of saying I am from Ukraine.'

The friendship between Oleksandr and Anton had been forged over many years as musicians around Kyiv, but now they are joined by a different bond. From this basement, they are both fighting the Russian army. Oleksandr looks to the world like a wild-haired musician who longs to be on stage – his presence in this basement is as incongruous as it would be to see Australian musician Nick Cave sitting in a Sydney or Melbourne basement making weapons of war. But we learn from Oleksandr and Anton that for them and so many other Ukrainians, the lives they thought they had needed must be put on hold until they rid themselves of what they regard as the cancer of Russia's occupation of one fifth of their country. They still exude all the charm, charisma and fun of musicians, but when the subject turn to Russians, they become focused and ruthless.

Nothing highlights this more strongly than when we ask Oleksandr if he has a message for Russians, once a people he performed for and shared vodka with. His anger is clear as he says in Russian, 'There is no vodka here – go home and fuck yourselves.'

*

In another part of Kyiv, an engineering lecturer is teaching his former students how to turn agricultural drones into 'gifts' for the Russians. I drive across town to meet Maxim Sheremet, a 27-year-old engineering graduate who's set himself up in an old warehouse. Along with scores of his students, he's begun making attack drones. The students ask farmers to donate agricultural drones that are normally used for spraying pesticides and then spend their nights turning them into military drones. When I visit the warehouse, the students are attaching cages to the bottom of the drones in which soldiers can pack explosives. Or, in the words of Maxim Sheremet, 'This is where we put the presents for the Russians.'

To walk around this warehouse nestled in an otherwise standard suburban shopping strip is a remarkable experience. (Maxim has asked me not to reveal the exact location as the

Russians would almost certainly target it if they knew this had become a major drone factory.) Inside is a smorgasbord of flying devices, from kamikaze drones the size of watermelons to drones almost two metres wide that look like gliders. 'We're helping our military by creating these birds for different applications in the army,' Maxim says.

As Europe's great 'food basket', Ukraine has thousands of farms and one of the world's biggest wheat industries as well as being a major producer of sunflower oil. Many of those farmers have donated to this group spare agricultural drones they'd been using to spray fertiliser on their crops.

The inventiveness of these adapted drones reflects the general creativity that Ukrainians have drawn on in this war. For example, Russia has probably put more landmines along the 1200-kilometre front line than have been placed along any other piece of land in history. To deal with this, Ukraine has repurposed agricultural vehicles to push long broom-like structures ahead of advancing troops, which will explode any mines fifteen or twenty metres ahead of the vehicle. If it weren't for the farmers donating their machinery, many more Ukrainian lives and limbs would be lost.

Sheremet has devoted his new life to making these drones. An engineering graduate and a lecturer, he's convinced as many as a hundred former and current students and colleagues to join his drone roster. Teams work from ten in the morning until ten at night with each group playing a part in the production line, from adapting the agricultural drones for attack to building cages. And it's not just his engineering students and fellow lecturers – everyday civilians 'with a good sense of aeronautics' have also joined the fight. He makes the point that his team is not particularly warlike by background or personality. 'A lot of people who work here actually cannot shoot a rifle, but they can do something with their hands,' he says. 'Some of them are not even yet eighteen years of age.'

Despite his own young age, Maxim is something of an engineering superstar in Ukraine. He not only lectures engineering students, some of whom are older than him, but is chief executive of a Ukrainian company. For several years he's been studying a specialist area: how to fly a drone without a GPS. Now, as part of the war effort, he's putting all his skills and smarts towards helping his country, attacking what he calls 'the pigs in the trenches'.

Until the war, this building we're in was a textile factory making clothes, but it has now been converted into a key part of Ukraine's war effort. Maxim gives me a tour of the warehouse. 'Right now you're in the drone lab,' he says. 'We're creating drones for our guys in the field. We create different drones for different tasks. In this lab work students and volunteers, all engineers. We have a lot of staff for creating big drones, planes and other research drones, kamikaze drones, whatever the army needs.'

Maxim has set up this laboratory so that the army can order online or come into the warehouse and choose their product. This takes off-the-shelf shopping to a new level. 'We have an online order form but ninety per cent of our sales are face to face. Friends tell friends that Maxim is creating cool drones, and the word goes around, and then the army comes in here. Guys come into my lab and say, "Maxim, we need drones for these tasks."'

Like Anton and Oleksandr's operation, Maxim's has different drones for different needs. Some of the drones here are for surveillance and research instead of death; in this case, the priority is the quality of the camera and its ability to swivel in any direction. Some are designed as first-aid responders with a medical kit attached. Some are designed to fly into buildings or people for instant destruction, the so-called kamikaze drones. And for the attack drones, they're fashioned to carry bombs that can destroy a tank or cause maximum damage to soldiers in a trench. Different bombs are chosen for different tasks.

The team here also makes drones called Banderyks, which have a thermal imaging camera that can detect the warmth of a human body, so the drone can still find Russian soldiers even if hiding under bushes or blankets. The army can then send in another drone to bomb the location from which the heat is coming. 'All are very efficient and show great results in the field,' says Maxim.

'Efficient' is one way to euphemistically put it. How does Maxim feel about the fact that some of these drones will kill people? 'Personally, like other engineers here, I am very proud that my drones are working on the field,' he says. 'Our mind is our gun. We do everything that we can to win this war. I'm very proud indeed that my birds are flying and doing these tactical tasks, because the main target for the engineer is that his product, his drones, are making these flights and help our country to win in this war.'

I ask him if killing Russians is part of the reality of war.

'Drones are not only killing, they're saving lives,' he counters. 'When our soldiers are trying to stay alive in trenches, they can't be firing guns at the same time. At that time, drones are able to do the shooting and so are saving lives as our soldiers don't need to put themselves in danger by coming out of the trenches. These drones are also giving our soldiers early warning of any incoming fire or attack.'

The tasks of the drones, says Maxim, change with the needs of the front line. 'At the first stage of the war we needed a lot of drones for artillery jobs and research jobs, also dropping medical supplies, dropping ammunition and so on. And as the war went on, we needed more kamikaze drones for attacking.' Maxim says the 'classic' kamikaze has a payload of only one kilogram of explosives. But his favourite drone is the Banderyk. 'They can carry an eight-kilogram payload and fly ten kilometres.'

Maxim says this is 'the world's biggest war of drones'. The team in this warehouse are students he was teaching when the war broke out. One of the classes he taught before the war was creating drones. For fun, once the students had built their own drones, he would take them to a park so they could all race their drones to see who had made the fastest. They hope one day to get back to drone racing.

But before that can happen, the university students in this warehouse have one very clear and focused mission: to force Vladimir Putin's soldiers from their country. And their motivation to survive by destroying the other side is kept alive by one man: their president, Volodymyr Zelensky.

CHAPTER 8

The leader: Zelensky

NOT LONG AFTER UKRAINE'S WAR WITH RUSSIA BEGAN, a 23-year-old sat watching the nightly television news with his mother in Maitland, a regional town an hour's drive from Sydney. Jack Jordan had his own business cleaning gutters and mowing lawns, was not particularly interested in international affairs and had never travelled overseas.

As this young man sat on the couch, Volodymyr Zelensky came on the television talking about his war with Russia. He said he needed people from around the world to help him fight the Russian army. Jack sat there transfixed. He listened to every word spoken by the Ukrainian leader. By the time the news item had finished, this young man had decided to fight a superpower on a distant shore.

This was the power of Volodymyr Zelensky.

'I saw President Zelensky's call for help, call for aid, call for foreign fighters, and I immediately knew that's what I was going to do,' Jack later tells me. It was, says Jack, a moral question. 'I think it just comes down to what's right and what's wrong. Good versus evil. I don't think there's been a war since the world wars that's this plain, plain as day, good versus evil ... I just think President Zelensky is taking Ukraine into the future, something that it hasn't seen before as a country, as a people. I think he's a strong man, and he's a man that I would follow.'

Indeed, he's a man that Jack Jordan *did* follow. To meet Jack, I head to a small village in eastern Ukraine, forty-five minutes' drive from the front line. Apart from the sound of a few chickens in the distance and some dogs watching me as I walk down an empty street, this village is more or less abandoned; most locals have fled as it's too close to the fighting. On the way here, in the forests surrounding this village, I see trenches built by Russian soldiers who've since been pushed back after claiming this land in the early weeks of this war.

As our van turns into a deserted street, I notice that there is much activity at one particular house. I learn later that Ukrainian soldiers come and go from here, having moved into this building and turned it into something of a refuge for relaxation when they need a break from the horror of the nearby front. As I wait, a four-wheel drive with soldiers approaches and out jumps a young, strong-looking man with tattoos. He extends a hand with the firm grasp one would expect from someone who's just come from a week on the front line. 'Jack from Maitland,' he says. 'You must be John from the ABC.'

Since leaving Australia, Jack Jordan has been spending his nights in a trench fighting the Russian army. He's clearly pleased to be meeting another Australian, even if it's a journalist. 'Not too many Aussies in this part of the world!' he says.

Jack wasn't sure how to tell his mother that he'd be going to Ukraine, so he tried breaking the ice in a light-hearted way. He cracked jokes about going to fight Putin, a difficult subject to make amusing, but his mother didn't take it seriously until the weeks leading up to his departure. 'She looked me dead in the eye and said, "You're really going, aren't you?" and I said, "Yes, I'm going."'

It's a new experience for me to meet someone from Australia who's gone to fight in a foreign war. So what does Jack say to friends or family who can't understand his decision? 'I tell them that I'm fighting for something that I believe in,' he says. If they still don't understand, he then asks them when the last time was that they fought for something they believed in. 'And the answer tends to be never,' he says. 'I'm living a meaningful life, fighting for a cause that I believe in.' And what cause is that? 'I believe that the Ukrainians deserve a life similar to what we get free in Australia. We all take that for granted, and

I want everyone to experience the life that I got without having to fight for it.'

Australians are prolific travellers, with Europe, the US and Southeast Asia being some of our favourite destinations, not regional Ukraine. I say to Jack that most 23-year-olds going overseas on their first trip don't end up fighting the Russian army. 'I think a lot of people my age live meaningless lives, where they value things that they shouldn't value, especially in Australia,' he says. 'In countries similar to Australia, we have everything given to us on a silver platter. It's easy to overlook what's happening in parts of the world that aren't so blessed.'

He's not the only one who has left a position of relative comfort for life in the trenches. While hundreds of thousands of Ukrainians joined the army, thousands of foreigners like Jack have come to Ukraine to join what's called the International Legion, a group of foreign fighters that battle alongside the Ukrainian army. For Jack, there was always something about joining an army that appealed to him. At seventeen he'd tried to join the Australian army but was rejected. 'I was associated with an outlaw motorcycle club, which is obviously frowned upon in Australia,' Jack says. He had been previously arrested and pled guilty to resisting a police officer and participitating in a criminal organisation.

It seems to me that part of the appeal of a group such as the International Legion is wanting to belong to something bigger than yourself, that band of brothers. Jack tells me that he's bonded strongly with a Canadian who sits twenty or thirty metres from him in another foxhole, and they spend their days off together.

'I consider them brothers,' Jack says. 'We don't let each other get down and think bad ways. It's definitely a brotherhood.' He agrees that's part of the appeal for him. 'I think what all men crave in a way is brotherhood, camaraderie, and that's exactly what we have here in Ukraine.'

When he's sitting in that foxhole at night with Russian tanks firing, does he ever think to himself, 'I'm a 23-year-old gutter cleaner from regional New South Wales – what the hell am I doing here?' 'Absolutely,' he says. 'You have nothing but time to think in that foxhole, and I've thought about everything there is to think about. That crosses my mind frequently, but it's always overshadowed by the cause, and truly believing in the cause, and that's why I'm here fighting.'

*

So who is Volodymyr Zelensky, a man with enough charisma to lure a lawn maintenance worker from suburban Australia to a freezing foxhole in Ukraine? Zelensky's story is an extraordinary one that in some ways reflects the story of the human condition. We all need to make choices, it's just that the choices most of us make don't usually alter the course of history.

Volodymyr Zelensky was born on 25 January 1978 in a working-class home in Kryvyi Rih, an industrial city in the south of Ukraine. Mention Kryvyi Rih to Ukrainians and they often start talking about crime and gangs. He grew up in a working-class Russian-speaking family. Perhaps the greatest irony of Zelensky's story is that a man who would put his life on the line for Ukraine had, until he was a young adult, been more fluent in Russian than Ukrainian.

Zelensky graduated in law from the Kryvyi Rih Institute of Economics, but law was never his love. He was, at heart, a performer. While studying law, Zelensky worked methodically to make a name for himself with his comedy troupe, Kvartal 95.

Though he loved all kinds of acting, he was drawn to comedy in particular and never looked down on it. A journalist who interviewed him years later said he would refer to Zelensky as an artist rather than a clown, but Zelensky objected. 'Why not?' he responded. 'Charlie Chaplin was the best of the clowns. He was a genius, and let's say in passing that he fought against fascism.'[15]

Few people could imagine such a dramatic career path, from clown to a leader charged with fending off the might of the Russian army. As French journalist Gallagher Fenwick observed in his book *Volodymyr Zelensky: Ukraine in the Blood*, 'Charlie Chaplin must become Churchill. Mastering the codes of digital communication which he uses to galvanise a resistance as fierce as it is delusionary in the face of the excess of a colossal aggressor, Zelensky becomes the face of a nation under siege and ready to fight.'[16]

Zelensky's preparation for being a wartime president wasn't borne out of a political science degree and decades of climbing the party ranks but from playing one on TV. Though it may feel like a fantastical leap from comedian to the leader of a nation, when you review the plot points in the years before his 2019 election, you can see what had seemed like an ad-hoc career path all came together.

In 2014, Ukrainians began protesting Russia's interference with their government. Thousands gathered in Maidan Square, Kyiv's central square, to express their anger at Ukraine's puppet Russian government. The crowds were protesting against the government's decision to suspend their country's association agreement with the European Union, which many Ukrainians thought would help to fight corruption in their country as well as turn their backs on Russia. But Ukraine's Russian-aligned President Yanukovych disagreed.

The protests turned violent in what became known as the Maidan Revolution. More than a hundred protesters were killed by riot police and snipers posted on rooftops. In the end, Yanukovych fled the country. As a final insult to Ukrainians, he'd been caught on CCTV stealing paintings from the presidential mansion before taking refuge in Russia, which many Ukrainians felt had been his natural home all along.

On 1 March 2014, ten days after the Maiden Revolution, Zelensky invited himself onto the 1+1 TV channel news show. Viewers quickly realised from the look on Zelensky's face that the actor had not come to entertain. Unlike many of his light-hearted comedic performances, on this evening Zelensky had an edge of seriousness when he faced the cameras with a blunt message. 'Mr Yanukovych, get out of the way.' Many Ukrainians who watched this felt it was the beginning of a serious political campaign.

In the life of Volodymyr Zelensky, 1 March marked a turning point. This was the first time he addressed the country without making jokes. There he immersed himself decidedly in the political arena. There the actor began his transformation.

In 2015, Zelensky began playing the Ukrainian president in a satirical TV show called *Servant of the People*. In the series, high-school teacher Vasily Petrovych Goloborodko – played by Zelensky – accidentally becomes leader of Ukraine after one of his students uploads a video of him raging about the state of corruption in Ukraine. It goes viral, and unbeknown to him, his students start a crowdfunding campaign to register his candidacy for president. Shockingly to everyone – most of all to Goloborodko, who's still living at home with his parents – he wins, becoming president of Ukraine.

Servant of the People ran for three seasons, from 2015 to 2019, and was extremely popular. As a profile by National Public

Radio highlighted, Zelensky had become a household name in Ukraine as a comedic actor, TV star, film producer and entertainment mogul, and his production company Kvartal 95 was at the time the biggest in the country.

In 2019 Zelensky ran for office, even naming his political party Servant of the People. But when Zelensky declared his candidacy for president, many Ukrainians thought he was not serious. He campaigned as the disruptor, the outsider prepared to challenge the establishment. Like his fictional presidential character, he also promised to eradicate corruption. French newspaper *Le Monde* reported on Zelensky's mindset: 'I'm the little guy from Kryvyi Rih and I came to break the system, defend Ukraine's European choice and finish the war [in Crimea].'[17]

Many Ukrainians were mesmerised by his performances, and his popularity grew throughout the campaign. He drew on all the skills he had developed as a performer, including delivering compelling speeches. He even challenged his rival and then-president Petro Poroshenko to a debate at the Olympic Stadium in Kyiv, which seats 70,000 people. But he did much more than this. He won the election.

On 21 April 2019, Zelensky was elected president of Ukraine. He won in a landslide with an extraordinary seventy-three per cent of the vote. His early months in office were promising. He formed a special court to deal with corruption, and his administration had such a sense of energy about it that it became nicknamed the 'turbo regime'. He limited parliamentary immunity for those charged with corruption and attempted to make land reform. Then he set about fixing the country's roads – Ukraine's infamous pot-holed streets had been a running joke on *Servant of the People*.

Zelensky was energetic and focused on reforms. He wanted Ukraine to be 'the state in a smartphone' – where a person could get a driver's licence, do their tax and carry out all other major transactions on their phone. He also wanted the digital systems to deal with corruption. The journalist Gallagher Fenwick notes that Zelensky also became a master of digital communication, which later, during the war, he used to rally the public. He says part of Zelensky's skill lies in his ability to use simple words to say weighty things and then spread those words far and wide. 'It resonates with his people before conquering the hearts and minds far from the borders of his country,'[18] Fenwick says.

According to Ukrainian media, Zelensky took on powerful people and institutions. His preparedness to take on supporters of Vladimir Putin quickly became obvious. He publicly challenged the broadcaster of 1+1 TV, an oligarch. Then he went after Viktor Medvedchuk's three television stations. Medvedchuk, a Ukrainian and one of Putin's closest friends, was identified by the United States intelligence community as someone who Putin hoped would take over from Zelensky. Medvedchuk would later be arrested by Ukrainian authorities before being handed over to Russia as part of a prisoner swap.

Putin had his friends, and Zelensky had his. Zelensky quickly surrounded himself with people he trusted. For example, he recruited his ex-roommate Sergei Shefir to become his adviser, and a friend from childhood, Ivan Bakanov, to become head of the SBU. Ukrainian media reported that about thirty people working for the government came from Kvartal 95 Studio, confirming that Zelensky valued people he had known for a long time and knew he could trust.

Many in Ukraine say his first two years as president were underwhelming. He was by several accounts disorganised, and Ukrainians were disappointed. His personal approval ratings collapsed. Many Ukrainians were wondering whether they may have placed all their hopes for leadership in someone who just didn't have what it took. An extensive profile in *Politico* reported that in the weeks leading up to Russia's invasion, senior Ukrainian opposition politicians and former ministers were brimming with frustration: 'They'd been imploring President Volodymyr Zelensky to meet with them – something he'd not done since his landslide election nearly two years before. They'd also been urging him to boost funding for the country's armed forces for months, clamoring for Ukraine's reservists to be called up as America's warnings of an invasion intensified – an invasion Zelensky still thought unlikely.'[19]

And then came the war. Overnight, Zelensky became the world's most famous leader. Overnight, he had the hopes of 44 million Ukrainians on his shoulders. He was becoming an increasingly unpopular politician, and not all politicians make great leaders. Could Zelensky be a modern-day orator like Churchill? Could he be a great military strategist like Napoleon? Would he one day be able to write his own version of Sun Tzu's *Art of War*, where he could outline the decisions he made that meant the difference between success and ruin? Or, at his essence, would Volodymyr Zelensky remain the wisecracking comedian who by sheer happenstance found himself in the vortex of history but could not rise above it when his country needed him?

History may well judge that Volodymyr Zelensky was a better leader than he was a politician. Putin's invasion forced a choice on Zelensky – a stark and very public choice. He'd been elected Ukraine's president by running as a cleanskin, a non-politician's politician who promised to take on Ukraine's notoriously corrupt political and financial systems. Suddenly, all his colourful, humorous campaign speeches, earnest plans to clean up corruption and promises to be a leader of the people became irrelevant. His job description changed overnight.

His country was at war and he was now a wartime leader. He was thrust into the role of having to defend his country against what was regarded as one of the most formidable armies in the world, tasked with winning the first major land war in Europe since World War II.

The Russian invasion was the fork in the road for Zelensky. As someone who had had an unorthodox path to high office, there were few indications as to how the comedian would act in the face of a challenge as big as a war. But as *Time* reported in their 2022 Person of the Year article, 'that experience turned out to have its advantages. Zelensky was adaptable, trained not to lose his nerve under pressure. He knew how to read a crowd and react to its moods and expectations. Now his audience was the world.' Zelensky had made clear his determination not to let them down. One example of this was his decision to stay in Kyiv, despite the risks of assassination, in order to make it more difficult for his subordinates to abandon ship.

In those first dramatic days, when Russian forces tried to storm Kyiv, Zelensky could have been spirited by helicopter from his own country, and many countries around the world would have given him asylum. History is full of leaders fleeing when extreme heat is applied. I remember as a young journalist being in the Philippines and watching an American helicopter dramatically extract the embattled dictator Ferdinand Marcos to safety as his own people came hunting for him at Malacañang Palace.

The United States raised the idea that Zelensky should run Ukraine's war effort from the safety of neighbouring Poland.

They even offered to set up a military headquarters in Warsaw, where Zelensky would enjoy all the protections afforded by the US and NATO.

Zelensky had more than just the Warsaw option. He could have fled to the US and made a lucrative career on the university and speaking circuit. He would have been paid vast amounts of money to talk about why the Russians were illegally occupying Ukraine or what the West could do to pressure Russia to end its occupation.

Instead he chose to stay and to fight. As he told US officials, 'I need ammunition, not a ride.'

So began one of the most extraordinary wars in history, Ukraine's battle to defend itself from the might and fury of Putin's Russia.

For the first few days after the invasion, Ukraine scrambled. Despite the build-up and threats from Russia, few in Ukraine thought Putin would go ahead with a land invasion. But after surviving those first few days, Ukraine was able to plan what would become one of the most impressive fightbacks in history. While Putin believed his army could march into Kyiv within days, Zelensky had other ideas.

Within Ukraine, he united the population; even his political enemies supported him. Outside Ukraine, he proved to be an extraordinary fundraiser: one day he was in Saudi Arabia with the Crown Prince, the next day in Italy or France. He used the international stage to amass one of the largest armies seen in Europe. Ukraine and Zelensky knew that when, inevitably, there would be negotiations, the stronger its military performance against Russia, the stronger its hand at the table.

Putin believed a successful invasion of Ukraine would do what Russia had been attempting for years – to obliterate Ukrainian culture and language, and to 'return' it to the Russian empire. But because of Ukraine's response, the belief that Ukrainians had in themselves soared. Ukrainians I spoke to during my three trips, particularly younger people, have stopped speaking Russian, instead taking pride in speaking Ukrainian.

The arrival of Trump was a godsend for Putin. Trump has always seemed intrigued by Putin, and seems to crave his respect. Putin seems to know how to play Trump – perhaps by personality; they are very similar and know each other's type. Two strong, ruthless men driven by power, who expect to get whatever they want.

Ukraine's single strongest desire was to join NATO, to give the country long-term insurance against any future Russian attacks. Three weeks after Trump returned to the White House, he telephoned Putin. It was the first conversation between a US and Russian president for two years. While parts of that call remained private, it's believed that during the conversation Trump guaranteed that Ukraine would not be admitted to NATO. That removed Russia's biggest obstacle to ending the war, and Trump and Putin decided to begin immediate peace talks.

Trump then rang Zelensky. The Ukrainian leader was on the back foot – the two big men had spoken without him. But Zelensky was not without guile. He'd long anticipated an unholy alliance between Trump and Putin, so had put in place his own insurance. Zelensky and his team had decided upon a strategy that they believed would appeal to Trump.

Ukraine has valuable rare earth and critical minerals in abundance, and the the US needs them for the defence, cyber and electric vehicle sectors. Should Trump not defend Ukraine, all these resources could fall into the hands of Russia.

Upon Russia's full-scale invasion, Zelensky adopted a military persona despite never having served in Ukraine's army. He held a media appearance to show Ukrainians that their leaders were staying in the country, so he did an army-style roll call. He called out the name of the country's prime minister, Denys Shmyhal, who responded, 'Present!' He then called out the name of the majority leader in parliament, Mykhailo Podolyak. 'Present!' he responded.

His media conferences were also like an early morning military assembly. At one, Zelensky told Ukrainians: 'As a president, I have no right to be afraid for myself – we've survived two world wars, three famines, the Holocaust, the Chernobyl explosion, the occupation of Crimea and the war in the east of the country. People have tried to destroy us many times unsuccessfully. So if anyone thinks that after overcoming all of this, Ukrainians will be broken and capitulate, then they don't know Ukraine and don't understand anything about Ukrainians.'

And if Ukrainians knew one thing, it was this: Zelensky was now the wartime leader they needed.

*

Wherever we went in Ukraine, we found real enthusiasm for Volodymyr Zelensky. He enjoys an unusual protected status for a politician in the modern era, when social media means that there's always somebody directing the worst possible criticisms at you. Zelensky is that rare breed of politician – both liked and respected.

Anastasiia Lebedenko, who we met earlier, typifies the view of many. 'I think he is an exemplary Ukrainian, that he is a person of courage and great strength and has showed it to us all Ukrainians who put trust in him every day,' she says. 'I think he is also a humble man. He is just doing his job and managing the war to the best of his ability, and I have huge respect for him, sacrificing his life, his energy, his advocacy, his family to do this. We see his presence, and it inspires so many people here and around the world.'

Olena, with whom Anastasiia was having coffee, says the most important thing that Zelensky has done is show the world that he's not scared. 'It would have been easier for him to have left the country, to go to the US, but he's shown us that we don't need to be scared,' she says. 'Zelensky has inspired us with his choice to stay in Ukraine, to travel to all these dangerous zones. He also has confidence, even in his eyes.' She tells us about a speech he gave on New Year's Eve 2023, during which she said many people cried because of the relationship he was creating with Ukrainians. 'He makes us feel that we are connected, that it is important to know who we are,' she says. 'It is important to trust him – he reflects our instincts that everything will be okay, that in the end, Ukraine will win. We need to be active and to do something and to be active about our choices, just like him.'

Anton Chernysh, the musician turned drone maker, says Zelensky has shown the world that Ukraine has courage. 'Even to the people of Ukraine, his actions [and] his public decisions have deserved respect,' he says. 'Usually Ukrainians would not respect any president, any government – they would be complaining that something is not right and so on. But President Zelensky has managed to get people united.'

And of course, there's the foreign soldier Jack Jordan, who found Zelensky's charisma so powerful that he left his lawn-mowing business in regional Australia to join Ukraine's fight for survival. After seeing Zelensky's appeal for foreign fighters, he went to the local post office and sent off his passport application. When that came back three weeks later, he booked his flights.

He flew into Poland and then tried to work out how to hook up with the foreign fighters. Finally he found the headquarters of the International Legion and joined. The legion was, of course, very keen to recruit as many people as it could – the idea of going to the front line to fight Russians does not appeal to most people of fighting age.

Whatever Jack had imagined as he sat on his couch at home in Maitland, the front was grim and confronting. 'Most of the time we're in foxholes, just by ourselves, we have nothing but time to think. It's very lonely, it's terrifying,' he says. 'A lot of the time there's nothing you can do, you just sit there waiting to die.'

Most nights Jack waits silently and alone only a kilometre or so from Russian soldiers in their trenches. Russian soldiers have been within a couple of hundred metres of him. As well as the main part of his foxhole, which is about two metres wide by one metre high, Jack has built a side tunnel in which he sleeps. He feels safer having this 'anteroom', because if the Russians fire a rocket near his foxhole, then instead of just having branches to cover him, he has the added protection of soil above him. The danger, of course, is that if the Russians fire a rocket that hits the soil above him, he could be buried alive.

Is he prepared to die? 'Absolutely,' he says. 'I'm terrified of dying. I don't want to die. Nobody wants to die. But I think it's a good cause to die for, to sacrifice yourself for. I think it's better to die fighting for something you believe in than just to live a life for instant gratifications and vices.'

Jack says that there is a big difference in the way that the Russian and Ukrainian armies treat their dead. 'I know for a fact that the Russian army does not collect their dead, it's not a priority of theirs,' he says. He's seen at least a dozen dead Russians, he says, 'Just abandoned, and some of them have been there since last year, they're completely skeletons.' By comparison, he says that the Ukrainian military values collecting their dead and their wounded. 'They will not leave you out there to die,' he says. 'And if you have died, they will send people out there under artillery fire to collect your corpse.'

With that daily fear that he could die at any moment, I ask Jack how he keeps his mental health strong. He says that's made easier by the people he surrounds himself with. 'There's a great morale in the Ukrainian military because they're fighting for something that they believe in,' he says. 'They're fighting for their home country. The morale is great, and we all keep each other up.'

Jack's roster with the International Legion is to spend one week at the front then have three days off. He has his own routine to decompress after a week on the front line. 'The first thing I do is shower, that's for sure,' he says. 'Then I brush my teeth. Hygiene is not a priority on the front line. Then I catch up on a lot of missed sleep.'

Did he ever think he would consider having a shower or brushing his teeth a luxury? 'Never in my life did I think they would be a luxury. Everything is within arm's reach in Australia, anything you want: food, shower, water,' he says. 'Those simple things are hard to find in Ukraine, especially on the front line.'

So what has sitting in that foxhole with the Russians a few hundred metres away taught him about himself and about life? 'I've definitely conjured up more bravery in the last couple of months than I've ever had to in my life in Australia,' he says. 'You're so protected in Australia. We're so far away from everything that happens in this part of the world. I've really got to know myself, spent a lot of time with myself and in my own mind.'

When you're immersed in the battlefield, it's difficult to assess who's winning the war. 'It changes on a daily basis. Every second, every minute, anyone could be winning at any given moment. I'd like to think Ukraine's winning, of course, because that's the side I'm fighting for.'

All this has stemmed from a speech Jack watched on the nightly news by a president who, at the beginning of the war, had spent more time playing one on TV than actually being one in parliament.

From the backblocks of Kryvyi Rih to a man holding the hopes of 44 million Ukrainians on his shoulders, Volodymyr

Zelensky is a compelling figure. The appeal that Jack Jordan felt is reflected among Ukrainians who daily take up arms to defend themselves against the Russian Army. But all that would not matter, of course, should Zelensky not be able to defeat Russia. To defeat Russia, he needed to understand Russia. And to understand Russia, Volodymyr Zelensky needed to journey inside the mind of Vladimir Vladimirovich Putin.

CHAPTER 9

The enemy: Putin

On 6 September 2013, Vladamir Putin and Barack Obama sat at a dining table in Russia's historic Grand Peterhof Palace near St Petersburg. It was one of the dinners that takes place during a G20 summit, which brings together the world's biggest powers to address issues relating to the global economy. Normally, major geopolitical changes occur slowly, and sometimes it's only later that we realise the significance of an event. But on this evening it was different. At this dinner, Putin made it clear that the world had changed. It was the warning shot for what would happen in Ukraine nine years later.

Seated next to Putin on the night the geopolitical order shifted was Bob Carr, Australia's then foreign minister. It was Russia's year to host, and as Australia was the host of the next

G20, protocol demanded this positioning. 'So I had Vladimir Putin on my left and on my right was Susilo Bambang Yudhoyono, the president of Indonesia,' Carr recalls. 'Next to him was Barack Obama.'

Australian prime minister Kevin Rudd was unable to attend, so he deputised Carr to go in his place. 'I was determined to enjoy the occasion,' Carr tells me. 'We were all at a circular table and we were served a stylish multi-course banquet by waiters in ceremonial eighteenth-century dress without the powdered wigs.'

Carr remembers that evening as if it were yesterday. Earlier, Putin had openly defied the United States, making clear that he no longer accepted Washington's influence on major international issues. Carr recalls Putin as super confident and Obama as meek, and that for the entire evening, there was not a single exchange between Obama and Putin. What struck Carr was that an American leader would put up so little resistance to Putin's declaration of a dramatically different world order. This was the world according to Putin.

The major theme of that G20 gathering was 'red lines' and who would enforce them. What had hung over the meeting was Obama's proposal that Syrian dictator Bashar al-Assad be hit with military strikes in response to his use of chemical weapons. The deployment of chemical weapons is widely considered a breach of international norms, and when reports emerged that Assad was preparing to use them against his own people, Obama declared this would be 'a red line'. There was the clear implication that the US would respond with military force. Assad was a close ally of Putin, and Putin wanted to ensure that Obama did not go ahead with any action against him. He also wanted to portray the US as weak, that it would threaten action but did not have the resolve to go through with it. Putin's view was that the days of American strength on the world stage were over.

The month before that dinner, Obama had decided the US would launch strikes on Syria. He'd convinced the UK and France to be part of such military action. French president François Hollande had jets ready on tarmacs around France, but according to French media, Hollande received a call from Obama asking him to delay; he wanted to talk to Putin first.[20] Hollande was furious. 'It was at this moment that Vladimir Putin realised that the decline of the West, the weakness of democracies, would allow him to advance as he wants,' he said.

Obama had blinked. He was seeing Putin the following month in St Petersburg at the G20 meeting and would tell him there that the US had decided to bomb. Obama had blinked once – would he blink again four weeks later in Russia?

Indeed he did. Obama had told advisers he would bring the issue of possible strikes against Assad to St Petersburg, something that mystified many observers because the likelihood that he would get endorsement from such a divided group was negligible.

Obama had talked tough in the lead-up to the dinner. He'd said, 'We have been very clear to the Assad regime, but also to other players on the ground, that a red line for us is we start seeing a whole bunch of chemical weapons moving around or being utilised.'

Obama's demeanour at the dinner, says Carr, was 'very cold'. Carr glanced sideways and was intrigued to see Obama pushing his food around his plate and, from what Carr could see, would not eat anything that appeared to have fat or sugar in it.

Making sure that Putin did not see him doing it, Carr scribbled a note to Obama and pushed it over to him. *You have Australia's support on your opposition to chemical weapons*, he'd written. *Assad's use of chemical weapons unacceptable*. Obama read it, then looked at Carr and nodded. 'He clearly appreciated the note,' Carr recalls.

At such gatherings, every leader is given the opportunity to say a few words. As host, Putin was permitted to choose the order of speakers. He determined that Obama would speak first and he would speak last. Obama summarised the US position on the war in Syria, saying he'd struggled to find solutions to the conflict in Syria without dragging the US into a war. Carr later wrote in his diary: 'He said Americans don't want war, his supporters don't want it even more than other Americans, but there's a need for what he calls "a limited, proportionate action that sends a message". He speaks of high confidence that chemical weapons were used and that the Syrian government was responsible. He says a violation of international law must have consequences.'

Carr says, 'My chief impression at the dinner was that Obama was wasting time in bringing the issue to the G20, primarily an economic forum. At least he was candid and admitted America was war-weary. But he must have known he wasn't going to get a ringing endorsement for retaliatory strikes against Assad.' Obama had blinked for the second time.

Putin went around the table, and one world leader after another spoke. Angela Merkel said, plainly, that she was about to face a national election and that given German public opinion, it was too difficult for her to support a military intervention in Syria. Italy's Enrico Letta said the Pope's comments against any escalation of the war was an impediment for him. It was clear that Obama's argument for tough action against Syria was not winning the key players in the room.

Putin then gave Bob Carr the nod. He stood and spoke against any use of chemical weapons. Australia had a long-standing view, Carr said, that chemical weapons were a breach of international norms. He pitched it as an independent, condemnatory view rather than merely echoing Washington's position.

Finally, the main event, the president of the Russian Federation. Putin's performance, says Carr, was 'surgical', devastating in its effectiveness. He did not miss his target: Obama. His comments were designed to demolish Obama's argument about possible action against Syria. Russia did not protect Assad, he insisted. Video materials did not prove anything, he stated. Chemical weapons that had been found in Aleppo were 'makeshift', suggesting they were not from Assad's government. He wrapped up his comments by saying, 'Let me read something that a candidate for the US Senate in Illinois once said about another military intervention in the Middle East.' The group of world leaders were enraptured as he proceeded to quote an aspiring Senator Obama vehemently opposing war in Iraq. 'What I am opposed to is a dumb war,' Obama said in his famous 2009 speech. 'What I am opposed to is a rash war.'

Obama did not look at Putin; he stared at his plate for the entire speech. Putin then quoted the Pope warning against military escalation. In the style of a lethal barrister, Putin had effectively adduced the words of two witnesses – Obama and the Pope – in his case against Obama. Carr observed later that the room was left with two overwhelming impressions: Obama had looked foolish in bringing an issue he did not have guaranteed support for to an economic forum, and Putin had looked at the top of his game.

Carr later made a diary entry:

Putin goes on, declaring actions outside the UNSC
[United Nations Security Council] are illegitimate and
that they 'cause chaos'. And then he concludes with
two very cunning debating points. He quotes what an
unnamed US leader said on one occasion about the
prospect of another intervention in the Middle East. He's
barely into it when I recognised the words as being those
of Obama himself, campaigning for the US Senate and
making a bid for the anti-war vote. 'I am against this hasty
war …' Then President Putin suggests we might listen to
the Pope and he quotes the letter from the Holy Father
about the need to avoid violence. Bang! Cop that!

That dinner was the last time Putin and Obama had any
contact. So badly did their relationship deteriorate that the
following year, when the two men were in Paris at the same
time, President François Hollande went to the extraordinary
length of putting on two dinners on the same evening: Barack
Obama arrived at the Élysée Palace for the 'first sitting', then
two hours later Putin arrived.

Putin must have taken Obama's meekness in St Petersburg as
a green light for both Russia's support for the Assad regime and
its increasingly aggressive actions in Crimea. Assad continued

to kill his own people, free from the threat of any US military action, and Putin continued his march towards Greater Russia.

Within months, Russian troops invaded Crimea with virtually no resistance. The Imperial War Museum noted that Russia took Crimea 'easily'. Once Crimea was taken, Putin set his mind to an invasion of Ukraine. Had Obama not blinked twice, Putin's plans might not have been actioned so swiftly.

After Obama put up no real fight in St Petersburg, Putin became increasingly contemptuous towards world leaders, even German Chancellor Angela Merkel, with whom he'd had good relations. In 2015 in Minsk, Putin was sitting up late with Merkel. About 1 am, Putin was refusing to admit there were Russian soldiers in the Donbas. As Laurent Fabius, then the French foreign minister, recalled: 'What I remember is suddenly Merkel, who had had enough, takes out a photo where you can see a Russian colonel in Ukraine in an occupied zone. Merkel says to Putin, "What's he doing, this colonel?" Putin looks at the photo, then at Merkel and says with a straight face, "He must have lost his way."'[21]

*

People often say that they wish they knew what was happening inside the heart and mind of Vladimir Putin. And in some ways, you can – by listening closely to what he says.

Those who have studied Putin say by examining some of his key speeches over twenty-five or so years, you can piece together a profile of a man who has changed history and wreaked havoc on parts of Europe. 'With someone like Putin or Hitler, it's often more simple than people think,' says former Australian ambassador to Moscow Peter Tesch. 'Look at what they say, do and write.' He gives the example of what Hitler wrote in *Mein Kampf* in 1925, which predicted his course of action. However, the difference is that Hitler was in opposition and had to seize power, whereas Putin already has it. 'Which means that it [is] easier for him to put into practice all the things [he's] been talking about.'

For example, Putin's speeches are frequently peppered with references to the grand days when Russian women had seven or eight children. Now, many Russians 'only' have three or four. So for him, taking twenty per cent of Ukraine's land was not just a successful expansion of Russia's unofficial borders but a big boost to its population. Russia may have a declining birth rate but his invasion of Ukraine would give Russia a population sugar hit of Russian speakers.

Another thing Putin often talked about as he was building his political career was the importance of 'rule of law'. Putin graduated in law from Leningrad State University and used the persona of a lawyer to give himself a political veneer, particularly on the international stage. The author of *Inside the*

Mind of Vladimir Putin, Michel Eltchaninoff,[22] says that Putin frequently made reference to his legal background to cultivate the image of a leader committed to due process and democratic institutions.

And strengthen them he did – for himself. When Putin was first made president in 2000, US president Bill Clinton looked hard into outgoing leader Boris Yeltsin's eyes. 'I'm a little bit concerned about this young man that you've turned over the presidency to,' he said. 'He doesn't have democracy in his heart.' How correct Clinton turned out to be.

Russian presidents are only meant to stay in power for a maximum of two terms, but Putin is currently sitting in the president's seat for the fifth time. In 2021, he signed a law that allows him to stay in power until 2036 when he would be eighty-three. This law reset his own term count but still limits any future president to two terms in office. Since he was elected in 2000, he has been in control of Russia for all but four years, when Dmitri Medvedev was president from 2008 to 2012, which makes Putin the longest-serving Russian leader since Joseph Stalin.

Putin knows never to be an ex-dictator. There are plenty of fringe benefits to being a serving one: choosing whatever wealth you'd like from government assets, a life of luxury, yachts and apartments around the world, and the best fringe benefit of all – no accountability. But being a dictator is the sort of job you need to hang onto; you have no option.

Communist dictator Nicolae Ceaușescu found this out the hard way in Romania in 1989, when it was still part of the Soviet Union. After his government was overthrown and he lost power, he and his wife, Elena, were executed by firing squad as they stood in a courtyard on Christmas Day. On the video of the execution, Ceaușescu can be seen weeping and begging for mercy. One of the men in the firing squad, Ionel Boeru later gave a sense of the brutality of it all: 'I shot them very fast,' he said. 'I feel I helped them to die with dignity.'

Some dignity, weeping beside a toilet block in a courtyard on a freezing Christmas Day. That image went around the world and almost certainly would have been burnt into the memory of another aspiring Soviet leader, Vladimir Putin. Like Putin, Ceaușescu once was all-powerful – the army, the government and the people did whatever he wanted. People feared him and his word was law. He could order the killing of whomever he liked, whenever he liked. One word to his security detail and they would kidnap or kill anyone who annoyed him. He possessed that intoxicating thing that few people ever have – absolute power.

So how has Putin held power for so long? Within Russia, Vladimir Putin's political survival has been built on strength through fear. Challenge Vladimir Putin without powerful and decisive backing and you're dead, says Russia expert Kyle Wilson, a longtime intelligence analyst. Now retired, Wilson used to write intelligence assessments for Australian prime ministers.

Three times Wilson was asked to interpret conversations between Putin and Australian politicians, including twice when then Prime Minister Tony Abbott spoke to Putin following the shooting down of MH-17, in which 38 Australians died. I ask how Wilson would describe Vladimir Putin. 'Mother's boy, fascist thug,' he replies, referring to a famous photograph of Putin as a boy on his mother's knee.

'The Russian word that best describes what drives Putin is *obida*,' Wilson says. 'This is a smouldering, visceral sense of resentment.' Wilson believes that bitterness was born when Putin managed to get into the organisation he worshipped, the KGB, but never reached its 'glamorous elite'. As a result, when he did finally take the ultimate power seat, he had something cruel to prove.

Wilson's analysis is that because of the invasion of Ukraine, Putin has become 'a pathological mass murderer, at ease with the blood of perhaps 500,000 on his hands, including thousands of children.' He not only rules the military now but also the political elite. Wilson says the Russian oligarchs are Putin's servants. 'They hold their wealth only so long as that suits him, because there is no such thing as private property in Russia: everything belongs to the state, and the tsar is the state,' he says. 'And the state is the law.'

It's impossible to know the true wealth of Vladimir Putin. His finances are very deliberately opaque. Putin has always had an eye on money-making opportunities – a close associate of Putin's began producing a brand of vodka named after Putin – Putinka. According to *The Moscow Times*, by 2005 this vodka was the market leader. And according to investigative website Proekt, Putin received profits of up to US$500 million from sales of the vodka and the use of his name.[23]

Putin, says Wilson, is very much a mafia figure – the *capo di tutti capi*. The way he speaks matches the brief. 'Have a look at Putin's scabrous language,' he says. '"Snot" is a favourite word. "Come to Moscow and we'll shorten your manhood, we're good at that," he said to a European Union journalist. "Scum and traitors … we need to cleanse the country of them, the way you spit out a fly that's flown into your mouth." This is his chosen language.'

Rhetoric is important to the Russian cause. Language unites, motivates, divides and derides. And as one of the masters of modern propaganda, Putin has weaponised it.

*

To try to maintain support within Russia for the war with Ukraine, Vladimir Putin needed to activate his extraordinary propaganda machine. Putin's propaganda can be illustrated by the way Moscow deals with its poor roads. Academic Vera Grantseva, a Russian who moved to Paris, says that in Russia, if people complained about roads, officials would publish manipulated images of holes in the asphalt being repaired. This system of 'permanent lies', she says, 'permeates all levels of power.'[24]

One of the propaganda systems Putin has championed is called Dialog, a state-supported social media network that carries uncritical articles about the successes of Russia and the failures of Ukraine. It gained notoriety in 2010 when it published a special calendar for Putin's fifty-eighth birthday, each month featuring a female journalism student in lingerie. Originally intended to make communication between government and citizens more effective, Dialog made people in the regions feel they had access to decision-makers. It took control of the social media accounts of Russian governors, regional minsters, state schools and even kindergartens. Independent online publication *The Bell* reported: 'Control over a plethora of state resources gave Dialog a ready base to spread propaganda.'[25]

As with any project that wins the support of Putin, Dialog is well funded; in fact, it receives more money than Russia's state television channel Russia-1, which airs a current affairs program every Sunday dedicated to the glory of Putin.

Putin's general propaganda machine takes George Orwell's dystopian novel *1984* to a new level, but it was met with some ironic resistance. Inside Russia, the owner of a small business made his own solitary protest by handing out free copies of Orwell's book to tell fellow Russians that the regime was lying about the need to invade Ukraine. Across Russia, sales of *1984* soared to the extent that Putin's regime felt the need to discredit the book, with Russia's foreign ministry declaring, 'For many years, we believed that Orwell was describing the horrors of totalitarianism. This is one of the world's great forgeries.'

But Putin was doing some forging of his own. He counted and recounted the recent referendum held in Ukraine, which, not surprisingly, given his control over counting in elections, showed that those polled wanted to be part of Russia. He spent much time trying to show Russians that the referendums he conducted to try to legitimise the annexation of Ukrainian territories were legitimate.

The propaganda worked so well that many Russians thought the Ukrainians actually wanted to be 'liberated'. Because of this successful campaign, some Russian soldiers sent to fight believed that the Ukrainians would welcome them into their cities. But instead of being met with open arms, the residents had armed themselves against them.

In one case, revealed on a soldier's text messages, a Russian mother talked to her son, Loush, minutes before he was killed. When she began the messages, the mother thought her son was still training as a soldier in Crimea. But in this final exchange between mother and son, it's clear that upon arriving to fight In Ukraine, he realised that the narrative he had been by the Russian media was all lies.

Mother: Loush, how are you doing? Are you really in training exercises?

Son: Mama I am no longer in Crimea. I am not in training sessions.

Mother: Where are you then? Papa is asking whether I can send you a parcel.

Son: What kind of a parcel do you want to send me?

Mother: Where are you?

Son: I am in Ukraine. There's a real war raging here. I am afraid. We are bombing all of the cities, even targeting civilians. We were told that they would welcome us – but they are falling under our armoured vehicles, throwing themselves under the wheels and not allowing us to pass. They call us fascist. Mama, this is so hard.[26]

A few minutes after Loush wrote those words, he was killed.

Another phone call broadcast by French broadcaster LCI between a young soldier in Ukraine and his brother in Russia illustrated the sheer wretchedness that soldiers were surprised to find at the front line.

Soldier: Yesterday on the front we had a big problem.

Brother: Were you bombed?

Soldier: No, one of us became completely mad and started firing at us and threw a grenade.

Brother: What, you killed him?

Soldier: He's sick. Yes, it was the commander.

Brother: Wow – you weren't hurt?

Soldier: No, I went to the side against a wall so as not to be shot. If it was up to me I would blow myself up with a grenade. It is unbearable here. Don't tell mama about my teeth please. All my teeth have fallen out. The teeth of most people here have fallen. They fall with their roots. There are only people without teeth here.

The Ukrainian front line was not the dream that the Russian media has sold. And if they tried to defect, they paid the price. Consider the ruthlessness of the way Putin insisted on the formation of Russian soldiers at the front. He decreed that there be 'enforcers', called *politruk*, who effectively formed a line behind the front-line troops. The role of these enforcers is to ensure that no-one from the front line can retreat if the battle becomes too gruesome. For this purpose, Putin drew on ex-KGB officers who have been trained to be merciless killers, a good indication of their preparedness to follow any order, including killing a fellow comrade if they try to leave.

In another well-known incident, Russian agents kidnapped a Russian defector who had fled the mercenary army Wagner to hide in Kyiv. After audaciously snatching him off the street in the heart of the capital of the enemy country, he was thrown into a van, taken to an unknown location and, once his kidnappers had set up their video camera, had his skull smashed with a sledgehammer. Asked about the killing, Wagner chief Yevgeny Prigozhin simply replied, 'A dog receives a dog's death.'

Different from Russia's official army, Wagner Group is a private army built as a Russian mercenary outfit – killers for hire. It is largely the creation of former hot dog salesman Yevgeny Prigozhin and military veteran Dimitry Utkin, who grew it into a US\$12 billion international empire. The business model of this group – a key part of Russia's war machine – was to earn income by providing 'security services' to international regimes such as that of Bashar al-Assad in Syria, from gold and diamond mines in Africa, and from being the conduit for arms dealing. All of this income came along with funding from the Kremlin for their efforts in Ukraine. Wagner also ran propaganda operations for Putin. They had a troll factory called 'The Internet Research Agency' in St Petersburg, which during the 2016 US election, ran a major disinformation campaign against Hillary Clinton.

Soon after Russia's invasion of Ukraine, Putin realised the Russian army was not as strong as he had believed and insisted that Wagner join the war effort. He gave them major financial incentives to join the war. He quickly came to rely on Wagner Group, giving Prigozhin enormous power. That power was on display for everybody to see when Prigozhin frequently belittled Russia's military commanders, who could do very little to answer back. Wagner troops put fear into any opponent, Ukrainian, Russian or otherwise.

Eventually, Prigozhin led a mutiny against Putin's Russian soldiers. Wagner fighters seized the city of Rostov, which was the supply base for Russian soldiers into Ukraine. They threatened to march on Moscow. Putin was clearly shocked and angry as he reinforced Moscow with tanks, describing Prigozhin's actions as 'a stab in the back'. It was the most serious threat ever to his leadership and was defused by Putin doing a deal allowing Prigozhin to take up exile in neighbouring Belarus. I remember watching this attempted mutiny and thinking that someone who so openly challenged the *capo di tutti capi* couldn't last long.

Two months later, Prigozhin took off from Moscow in his private jet with several of his most trusted Wagner advisers. A few minutes after take off, the plane dropped from the sky like a stone, careering headfirst into the ground and killing all on board.

Yet another Putin rival was dead. The Kremlin denied any role and Putin expressed his condolences. But he added one observation: Prigozhin, he said, had 'made serious mistakes in life'.

The Godfather had spoken.

*

Russia's former world chess champion Garry Kasparov has a blunt analysis of what his country has become. 'Don't wonder what will happen if Russia collapses,' he once said. 'It already did. Years ago. It's not a state, it's a mafia front with factions fighting each other for money, resources and power. It's therefore no surprise that the man atop that mafia state has a certain paranoia about his own safety.'[27]

It should be clear by now that Putin has made many enemies who would like to see him dead. Safety is therefore of the utmost importance to the Russian president. Most world leaders have tight security, but it's arguable that none has security like Vladimir Putin. Not only does Putin have KGB culture in his DNA, he's assembled around him a praetorian guard of other former KGB, Federal Security Service (FSB) and military intelligence (GRU) officers who protect him.

Vladamir Putin lives in a bubble. 'Remember, he's the tsar, so he's isolated,' says Kyle Wilson, the Russia expert. 'He can't afford to have friends.' He does not read newspapers nor the internet. He only watches state news programs that recycle his views. He gets almost all his information from the red files left on his desk. His approach to media consumption resembles the protective iron curtain that he has drawn around himself both mentally and physically.

Putin's security tells part of the story of his psychology. If you work for Putin, you are not permitted to hold a current passport.

This is to ensure that should you try to kill him, you would not be able to leave Russia. He has at least three body doubles, men who look so much like him that when they turn up to functions, often people do not realise it is not Putin. He's even set up several offices around the country to look identical to his main Kremlin office so that nobody can tell from which location he's speaking when he delivers addresses to the nation.

When he needs some time out from running a war, he has many dachas – country retreats – around Russia, but his main one reveals his extraordinary security. Known as 'Putin's Palace', it sits on over seventy-four hectares of land on the Black Sea coast of southern Russia, has a no-fly zone covering the entire region and is surrounded by seven thousand hectares of forest. Longtime observers say the area makes Putin feel safe because a mountain is behind him and the sea in front. He also has neighbours he can trust in former president Dmitry Medvedev and security chief Alexander Bortnikov.

In 2010, Sergei Kolesnikov, a Russian businessman and whistleblower, wrote an open letter to then president Dmitry Medvedev regarding corruption in Russia and specifically about the construction of 'Putin's Palace'. Kolesnikov alleged that US$1.37 billion of public funds were used to build the palace. He fled Russia soon after writing the letter.

In 2021, the late Putin critic Alexei Navalny released a video about the dacha, stating the grounds were thirty-nine times the size of Monaco. Some of the locals claim the forest is so heavily mined that no-one goes anywhere near it. The dacha has helipads, a hockey ring, a bar, a casino, eleven bedrooms and a bomb shelter. There's a 'men's club' with stripper poles, guest houses and a church. It has a dormitory for staff and security. No-one is allowed on the property with a mobile phone or a camera.

In 2023, one of Putin's former security guards who escaped to Ecuador described the dacha as a mini city, with a gym whose instructors were all attractive young women, an upmarket tea salon and a private beach. It has a pool, two tennis courts and a full-size opera concert hall. Two weeks before Putin visits the dacha, said the guard, it's visited by Putin's personal security detail. A specific person is designated for specific roles – for example, only one person is permitted to turn on the washing machine. One person to open the garage. One person to open the front security gate.

When the real Putin is due to visit, no boat is allowed to enter the bay. He has a tunnel from the dacha to the beach, so if he wants to swim, he does not need to walk across land. If Putin decides to have a dip, agents swim five metres from shore to make sure that there's no-one hiding under the water. When he's swimming, no boats are allowed near him. Russian commando frogmen patrol the beachfront. Because of body doubles, even staff don't always know whether the person they see in the distance is really Putin. This all makes an assassination attempt extremely difficult.

In case there is a suspected attempt on his life, under the dacha runs a network of tunnels with sealed rooms with ventilation and supplies on which Putin and his family could survive for months. In 2021, journalist Mattathias Schwartz of *Insider* received information that the dacha had an elevator shaft leading to a bunker below, which has an intricate cable system guaranteeing power and communication.[28] As well as a self-contained power supply, the bunker has sewerage and water systems. There are two tunnels, one leading to the beach and the other to a road that would be an escape route if Putin needed to flee. The walls of the bunker are reinforced concrete, and the tunnels have been designed to protect Putin should there be a chemical or any other attack.

Through his propaganda, political power and physical property, Putin has made himself untouchable; people who try often end up mysteriously dead. Even the world's most respected modern leaders can't land a political blow, and some critics say that's what emboldened Putin to invade Ukraine in the first place. It was true of Obama, and it's been true of the six other US presidents who have tried to crack Putin.

*

It's an indication of Putin's longevity that his career has spanned seven different US presidents. The US investigative television program *Frontline* tracked Putin's relationship with all seven, beginning with Ronald Reagan. At the time of Reagan's presidency, Putin was a young KGB officer. As an ambitious Soviet spy, Putin watched as Reagan stood at the Berlin Wall and declared, 'Mr Gorbachev, tear down this wall!' *Frontline* observed that the collapse of the Soviet Union, spurred on by an American president, was a humiliation.[29] As Marie Yovanovitch, political officer at the US embassy in Moscow from 1993 to 1996 observed, 'You can only imagine what it must have been like as a young KGB officer. Your country disappears or is in the process of disappearing … It must have been devastating.'

That would be the first of many humiliations Putin would feel from a US president. The next came from George HW Bush, with his celebration of the end of the Soviet Union: 'It's a victory for the moral force of our values.' Then came Bill Clinton, Putin's least favourite president. American journalist Peter Baker says Putin was 'a cold fish' at their first meeting.

Next was George Bush Jr, who for a short time had what the US media described as a 'bromance' with Putin. After their first meeting at Bush's ranch in Texas, Bush was convinced they had a special relationship. One journalist asked if Putin was a man who Americans could trust: 'I looked the man in the eye,' Bush responded. 'I found him to be very straightforward. I was able to get a sense of his soul. He's a man deeply committed to his country and the best interests of his country.' But Russian journalists, knowing Putin, realised he'd won the exchange. Russian journalist Yevgenia Albats told *Frontline*: '[Putin] was trained not to reveal his, so to say, "soul", if he has any. His life experience didn't allow him to reveal any inner him, any true him, to any representative of the West.'

Any 'special relationship' was blown apart with Bush's decision to begin the Iraq war. As *The New Yorker*'s Evan Osnos observed, 'Vladimir Putin concluded that the United States, when possible, would use its power and leverage to depose leaders that it did not agree with. And from Vladimir Putin's perspective, that was an existential threat.'

Putin made his anger at the West clear at the Munich security conference. 'First and foremost,' he said, 'the United States has overstepped its national borders in the economic, political and humanitarian spheres it imposes on other nations. Well, who would like this? Who would like this? This is, of course, extremely dangerous. It results in the fact that no-one feels safe.' Former US Deputy Secretary of State Strobe Talbot said later on *Frontline*, 'My head snapped. It was so searing and blunt, and I felt this was the real guy.'

Putin was on the prowl. He audaciously turned up to a dinner of NATO members so he could confront Bush. As The New York Times' former Moscow correspondent Peter Baker told Frontline, 'He has basically shown up as the skunk in the garden and challenging them for what they've done.' He knew that the major focus of the meeting was Ukraine and the desire by the US in particular to bring it into NATO. According to the US ambassador to Ukraine from 2006 to 2009, Putin leant over to Bush and said, 'Ukraine is not a real country.'

Feeling emboldened, Russia attacked Georgia. That year, both Putin and Bush attended the Olympic Games in Beijing. Although not originally seated together, journalist Peter Baker said Bush asked his wife, Laura, and the King of Cambodia to move positions so that he could sit next to Putin. '[Bush] knows the cameras are on him, so he's trying not to make it a big visible confrontation,' Baker said. 'But he's telling Putin, "What are you doing here? This is not right. You can't be doing this." And Putin is basically telling him to butt out.' An adviser from the US National Security Council, Thomas Graham, would say later on *Frontline*, 'I remember the president saying, "You know, I don't know how, but we've lost him."'

Those words – 'we've lost him' – would ring true. Putin set his sights on the two big prizes he coveted, Crimea and Ukraine. At his first meeting with Obama, Putin was passive-aggressive, with a short question from Obama resulting in a 45-minute answer by Putin. So dysfunctional was the relationship – some observers said later that they believed a racist Putin resented having to speak to an African American president – that

Obama 'handed over' Russia to his vice president, Joe Biden. In his memoir, Biden described Putin as 'ice-cold calm' at one of their meetings: '"I'm looking into your eyes," I told him, smiling. "I don't think you have a soul." He looked at me for a second and smiled back. "We understand each other," he said. And we did.'

Unlike his relationships with other US presidents, Donald Trump and Putin actually did have a special rapport. Stephen Hadley, US national security adviser between 2005 and 2009, told *Frontline* that Putin's view of Trump was 'a penchant for authoritarianism, a backing off of human rights and talking about wanting to have a more positive relationship with Russia. What's not to like if you're Vladimir Putin? It sort of sounds like he's one of us.' Journalist Peter Baker said of Trump's victory that not only did the candidate Putin favoured win but he had also disrupted Americans' faith in their own democracy, 'so that we're all turning on each other and we're busy fighting with each other and in [Putin's] mind hopefully too distracted to pose a threat to him on the world stage.'

And as to the chaos on Trump's election loss, author Timothy Snyder told *Frontline* that nobody loved the 6 January mob attack on the US Congress more than Russia. 'Trump gave them four years, which was one big gift, but January sixth was like the wrapping, the beautiful wrapping, the package.'

And, after four years of Joe Biden's presidency, which

resumed a relationship formed in the Obama era, the leader of the Russian people hoped he'd finally get to open that present.

*

In my three trips to Ukraine, what struck me more than anything else was how focused Ukrainians were on the US presidential election of 2024. To the outside world, it seemed Ukrainians were primarily focused on Russia. Of course Ukrainians follow developments in the Kremlin closely, keeping a keen eye on anything that indicates a change in strategy or funding for Moscow's war effort. But from soon after the 2022 Russian invasion, Ukrainians repeatedly said that the American election of 2024 would be decisive.

In particular, they were fixated on one candidate: Donald Trump. Would Trump return to power? They knew enough from his public comments that he had far less respect for NATO than most influential Democrats and many senior Republicans. And without a strong NATO, Ukraine was in deep trouble. Ukrainians knew that on their own, they were no military match for Russia. A second Trump term could spell the end of the war – but not in their favour.

Trump had made one comment in particular that rocked many Ukrainians. In May 2023 he told CNN's Kaitlan Collins, 'If I'm president, I will have that war settled in one day, twenty-four hours.' When pushed on this by Collins, Trump added that he would bring together Vladimir Putin and Volodymyr Zelensky. 'They both have weaknesses and they both have strengths, and within twenty-four hours that war will be settled, that war will be over.'

The overwhelming sentiment of Ukrainians I spoke to about this comment was that they were worried that Trump would insist that Putin and Zelensky bring the war to a close, and that each side would keep whatever land they had at that time. This would reward Putin as he has taken almost twenty per cent of Ukraine in the three years since the Russian invasion.

Zelensky himself reflected that fear when he responded to Trump's comment. In an interview with Britain's Channel 4, he said he thought the twenty-four-hour comment was 'very dangerous', adding that it could be electioneering. Nonetheless, Zelensky's response gave expression to a deep fear among Ukrainians about the 2024 election. While the battle between Donald Trump and Kamala Harris was one of the most watched US elections in history, it gripped Ukrainians more than most. For them, this was not just a fascinating struggle for the direction of the United States but also about their possible survival as a sovereign country. If Trump won and forced a deal under which Ukraine unilaterally lost a fifth of their land, the consequences within Ukraine would be devastating. Ukrainians would most likely turn on each other, unleashing a possible civil war. Many Ukrainians would ask, 'Why have hundreds of thousands of our soldiers been killed or disabled just to hand the territory to Putin?'

*

The future of Ukraine as the world knows it is now in doubt. In 2024, Trump led the Republican party to victory in the White House, the House of Representatives and the Senate. He is now the most powerful US President since Franklin Delano Roosevelt. Adding to this power is the fact that, given that a US president cannot run for a third term, Trump never again has to face voters. Trump roared into a new term with none of the political limitations of a first-term president.

Donald Trump could now decide the future of Ukraine. Will he force Ukrainians to accept a ceasefire under which they lose one-fifth of their country? Or will he decide that he could write himself into history as the all-powerful leader who took on Vladimir Putin and backed Ukraine to the hilt?

Trump had made his name telling people 'You're fired!' on reality television and doing deals as a Manhattan property developer. In one of the most unlikely twists in modern history, Trump now holds the key to the future of Ukraine.

Could re-drawing the map of Europe be Donald Trump's ultimate deal?

CHAPTER 10

The deal maker: Trump

IT'S TWO DAYS AFTER DONALD TRUMP HAS RE-TAKEN THE White House and Sylvie and I are in Ukraine House in Washington, a key meeting place for members of the Ukrainian community in the United States. A Ukrainian woman who regularly visits the centre is talking to visitors about the Russian cultural centre down the road, and whether Russian spies ever come to events at Ukraine House to find out what's happening in the Ukrainian community. Some Russians, of course, speak Ukrainian, as do many Ukrainians speak Russian. 'But when Russians speak Ukrainian they cannot always get the accent perfect,' the woman says. 'There's a few words they just can't pronounce, words that always trick them up!'

One of those trick words is *palianytsia* – the Ukrainian word for a loaf of round bread. It's a quirk, but for some reasons Russians – no matter how much they try – find it hard to pronounce the word. Ukrainians laugh about how it always gives away a Russian pretending to be Ukrainian.

Just down the road – between Ukraine House and the Russian Cultural Center – is the French Embassy. It has a replica of the Statue of Liberty in its front yard and from the first days of Russia's invasion of Ukraine in 2022 the embassy has wrapped the statue in the Ukrainian flag. In this town, where every country fights for influence and goodwill, this is an unmistakable show of support for Ukraine.

For Ukrainians in Washington, being on guard for Russian spies has been part of their life since Russia's invasion of Crimea in 2014. So has been their mission to try to keep the United States supporting their war against Russia.

There is a widespread view in Washington that Putin and Russia play hard and dirty. This perception was confirmed two days after Trump won power – Russia's most watched news program showed nude pictures of Melania Trump, claiming it was a form of 'welcome' for Trump. It seemed more like something straight from a Mafia playbook – not quite a horse's head in a bed, but not far off. There was a real hint by the Russian media that 'these are the photographs we have of Melania – and we may have more'.

As Russia plays its propaganda tricks, Washington is replete with Ukrainians boosting their country's profile. One of those is Ruslan Falkov, who had been a diplomat with Ukraine's embassy when he decided to open the city's first Ukrainian restaurant. After there was publicity that the restaurant was about to open, the venue was burnt down. Falkov has his suspicions about who may have lit the fire, but does not have proof so prefers not to publicly speculate.

He was not daunted, however, and now owns two restaurants in Washington. The restaurants have become gathering places for the Ukrainian community, as well as drivers of fundraising. The programs Falkov has run include one for children who have lost limbs and need prosthetics. Fundraising has provided indefinite care for the children, including flying them from Ukraine to the US whenever they need medical treatment. Because children grow quickly, sometimes they need prosthetics adjusted once or twice a year. Among the children in the program are Daryma, a six-year-old from Nikopol who lost her legs when a Russian missile hit her home, and Sasha, nine years old, who was in a car with her parents on the third day of the war trying to flee the family home in Hostomel when their car was hit.

One thing that is absolutely clear from our time in Ukraine is that Ukrainians will never surrender. Dr Olga Boichak is a Ukrainian-born senior lecturer in Digital Cultures at the University of Sydney. She says the resistance Ukrainians have demonstrated in recent years is a continuation of an important historical process that has been ongoing for more than 100 years. 'This speaks to the fact that Ukraine's nation is much older than the thirty plus years as an independent state, and gives Ukrainians energy and determination to continue the fight.'

Dr Boichak says the war has been going on since Russia's invasion of Crimea – and that Ukraine has suffered heavy losses and devastation but demonstrated unprecedented levels of resistance and resilience. 'Amidst a less-than-optimistic prognosis and deteriorating living standards, Ukrainians have been defiant agents of social, cultural and economic change in their country.' The war has changed Ukraine, she says, because there is now a better understanding of, and resistance to, 'Russia's expansionist cultural politics, which were an element of its occupation strategy. There are also much higher levels of media literacy and awareness of adversary influence operations in the society.'

She says that Ukraine's Armed Forces also underwent a remarkable transformation driven by the volunteer movement – evolving from 'a poorly functioning, corruption-ridden institution burdened by its Soviet legacy, into a motivated, well-trained and significantly better-equipped fighting force.'

It is now, she says, one of the most innovative and best-trained armies and utilises unique forms of military–civilian relations that would be of interest to Ukraine's allies.

'Some groups in Ukraine have expanded their range of activities to include delivery of automobiles and high-tech equipment (such as FPV drones and night-vision heat detectors) while others specialise in tactical medicine and evacuation. A number of groups across the country provide service delivery to veterans and their families, while others started implementing initiatives on the digital battlefronts, from database software and cyber counterattacks provided by the country's growing IT sector, to the creation of high-precision tactical GIS maps for the military – a collaborative effort that involved over a hundred Ukrainian cartographers.'

Whether formal or informal, volunteering contributes to the creation of new norms and values of citizenship in Ukraine, says Dr Boichak, bridging demographic and cultural divides and strengthening the social fabric. 'We saw displaced persons become actively involved in these initiatives in their new places of residence – whether in Ukraine or overseas, including here in Sydney. Many see it as a way to break away from Ukraine's past and contribute to the shaping of contemporary Ukraine as a democratic, prosperous, and diverse nation – a version of civic national identity that's so distinct from the ethnonationalist representations propagated by the Russian Federation.'

*

One of the reasons that Sylvie and I conclude as to why Ukraine is slowly losing this war – despite having NATO and US backing – is that the US has gone deliberately slow on delivery of weapons to ensure that Russia cannot lose. This has spared Putin being humiliated and either lashing out, possibly with a nuclear weapon, or being replaced by a less predictable leader. Better the tyrant you know.

Retired Australian Army General and Senior Fellow for Military Studies at the Lowy Institute Mick Ryan says there's no doubt that a certain fear had slowed decisions to support NATO. 'Joe Biden has repeatedly referred to a third world war,' Ryan says. 'Indeed, I believe he has been obsessed with this to the exclusion of all other strategies that might have guided US behaviour in the past three years. It has seen the US argue that providing normal conventional weapons such as artillery, air defence and tanks, used by the Russians since day one of the 2022 invasion, were escalatory. Indeed, the Biden administration have demonstrated a form of "escalation terror" throughout the war, and it has slowed decision-making about support in NATO, slowed support getting to Ukraine and constrained the quantity and types of support provided. It is also fair to propose that in the first year or two of the war, many in the US strategic community were afraid of a Russian collapse and loose nukes.

Therefore, many in the Biden administration and the wider national security community were more scared of a Russian defeat than a Ukrainian defeat, at least until the middle of 2023. By this time, however, Russia had recovered from the missteps that might have been exploited by a larger, faster program of western aid in the preceding eighteen months, and particularly in the first six months, when the strategic community was obsessed with debate over whether tanks were escalatory. Rather than a strategic success evidenced by a reinvigoration of NATO, this will probably be seen in the medium and long term as a major strategic failure by America and NATO.'

After following the Ukraine war for three years and spending time in Kyiv with key defence and intelligence figures, my conclusion is that the United States *did* fear Russia, particularly because of its nuclear arsenal. Understandably, Washington did not want the war to escalate. Putin consistently raises the spectre of nuclear weapons, which many people dismiss, but how can anyone know what's in the mind of Putin? As a result, my view is that the US carefully staggered the delivery of key weaponry, not wanting to overly anger Putin. They also did not know what might come next. This is why Ukraine did not win. The available evidence suggests that the US did not want Putin to win – but neither did they want him to lose.

For six years American diplomat John Sullivan had extraordinary insights into Russia and the mindset of the

Kremlin – he saw all the most sensitive intelligence. Sullivan saw the Russian build-up to the 2022 invasion of Ukraine over four years as US Deputy Secretary of State and then two years as US Ambassador to Moscow, and he was in Kyiv when Russia launched its full-scale invasion.

Based on all the material Sullivan read, he agrees with other commentators that the Biden administration deliberately went slow on delivery of crucial weapons for Ukraine for fear of provoking Putin. In his memoir, *Midnight in Moscow*, he writes that the administration did not do enough to provide weapons systems such as missiles, tanks and aircraft to Ukraine. That is no way, he says, to support a fellow democracy under attack by a much larger, aggressive, authoritarian foe. He agrees that Biden's hesitancy reveals a 'fear of provoking Putin to widen the war and attack NATO or use a tactical nuclear weapon'.

The brutal political reality is that the long-term future of Ukraine and the war will be decided in Washington – not Kyiv or Moscow. For many in the US, support for Ukraine is much more than just a battle against an expansionist Russia – it's seen by much of the defence and intelligence community as a way to send a message to China that any aspiration to invade Taiwan will be met with a similar level of support as that given to Ukraine.

Peter Tesch says the post-1945 US-dominated global order has been 'squarely in Moscow's sights' since Putin denounced it in his speech at the 2007 Munich Security Conference. Xi Jinping's increasing assertion of China's interests contributes to this sustained assault on US primacy. As Tesch says, 'Both leaders perceive a lack of resolve on the part of the West, evident in the relatively muted reaction to Russian aggression in Georgia in 2008, in Donbas, and particularly its illegal annexation of Crimea in 2014. The hollowness of Obama's [2015] warning that chemical weapons use in Syria would be a "red line" reinforced this view, as did Trump's willingness to cut a deal with the Taliban (bypassing the government in Kabul), which was the basis for the precipitate US withdrawal from Afghanistan under President Biden. These events have strengthened Moscow's and Beijing's conviction that America's convening power and commitment to global leadership is irreversibly waning.'

David J Kramer is a former assistant secretary for Russia and Ukraine in the US State Department. He told us that, should the US abandon Ukraine, 'Putin's appetite would grow with the eating' and he'd threaten other countries in the region, including possibly NATO members. 'China would interpret a withdrawal in support for Ukraine as a signal that maybe it could get away with an attack on Taiwan. Ukraine has never asked us to send our men and women to fight this fight for them, but they do very much need our assistance.'

Kramer cautions against judging a second Trump administration on comments made by Trump and other

Republicans during the presidential election campaign. He says the new administration has an opportunity to get some things right that the Biden administration failed at: an expedited decision-making process to get Ukraine what it needs, lifting restrictions on what the US provides militarily, inviting Ukraine to join NATO and seizing, not just freezing, Russia's US$300 billion in assets left in western financial institutions. The new administration, he says, will likely face a Putin who is not serious about negotiations and that will influence the new team's approach.

He pushes back against commentary that the American public is questioning why the US is funding Ukraine. 'I think there is broader support among Americans for helping Ukraine than many think. Once people hear the explanation of why it's important to support Ukraine, I think approval for doing so will be sustained, if not rise. Helping Ukraine regain momentum on the battlefield will also help. Everyone likes a winner and we should want Ukraine to win this war and defeat Russia.'

Donald Trump is famous for liking winners. And few presidents have had the level of impact as Trump before they've even walked into the Oval Office. Even as he sat in Mar-a-Lago mansion with Elon Musk, waiting to return to the Oval Office, the Trump Effect kicked in and he was impacting the Ukraine battlefield.

Once it became clear Trump was heading for victory in 2024, both Ukraine and Russia changed approaches. Ukraine made an audacious takeover of the Kursk region of Russia to try to give itself a bargaining chip at any Trump-brokered negotiations, while North Korea rushed an estimated 10,000 soldiers to try to help Russia retake it.

In terms of US public opinion, surveys consistently show that Americans see Russia as a real threat to Europe and world peace. Says David Kramer, 'Russia is a threat not only to its neighbours but to our allies elsewhere around the globe and to us here at home, whether through election interference, cyber attacks, including during a pandemic, disinformation, transnational repression, even sabotage attempts. Putin and his regime mean us harm and it's important that we recognise that.'

Retired general Mick Ryan says that after three years of war Russia has 'strategic momentum'. He says, 'Ever since the failure of the Ukrainian counteroffensive [in 2023], Russia has sought to implement a new strategy of generating momentum on the ground, and in the minds of western decision makers, regardless of the cost. While this has translated into hundreds of thousands of casualties for the Russians, they have had some success in reinforcing their partnerships with China, Iran and North Korea, while also convincing some in the American polity that coercing Ukraine into a ceasefire is a good thing.'

Ryan says neither the US nor NATO has produced an effective strategy for countering the Russian invasion, and that is part of Ukraine's challenge. 'While Ukraine welcomes statements about support "for as long as it takes" and allocations of financial, military and other forms of aid, the lack of a western strategy means that Ukraine does not really know what the West wants from the war. Does it want Ukraine to win? Neither of the candidates for the US presidency would answer this question before the election. Does it want Russia to lose? Biden has been clear that his objective is first and foremost to avoid World War III. This lack of a clear strategy is actually a strategy for defeat.'

In contrast, says Ryan, Russia had a clear strategy from the start: to subjugate Ukraine. While its methods might have evolved, it has stuck with this strategy for the entirety of the war and has adapted it when required.

'Therefore there remains a vast gulf [between Russia and the West]. While Ukraine has agency, and is doing all the fighting, unless the West moves from its "as long as it takes" slogan to a strategy that embraces a Russian defeat in Ukraine, it is hard to see a war termination that is favourable for Ukraine. But at the same time, it is easy to see a more confident, encouraged and aggressive Russia making Europe pay for its fickleness and lack of commitment in the past three years.'

Ryan has no doubt that Russia is running extensive black ops against various countries. 'Russia has an active campaign of sabotage and malign influence in multiple nations across Europe. From poisoning dissidents in the UK, to fires and other sabotage in Poland, France and elsewhere, this deniable campaign is designed to send a message to western politicians to not challenge Russian influence, while it is also calibrated by the Russians to not go too far and elicit a significant response. This is absolutely no surprise for anyone who studies Russian ways of war. Their unconventional operations in Europe are a core part of their military doctrine, as it is China's. The big surprise is that we have been surprised by them doing what they said they would do in their military doctrine.'

Russia's use of 'black ops' against various countries, says Peter Tesch, may well prove to be a bigger and longer-term challenge than the risk of direct military conflict. 'We have been slow to grasp how adept Moscow is at working with the grain of our societies, exploiting the inherent fractiousness of democracy. Contestability and debate are at the heart of our government and policy-making. By distorting, falsifying and manipulating information, the Kremlin seeks to amplify discord and widen the fissures in our societies, including by fomenting mistrust in the intent and integrity of government. Turning us against ourselves creates more room to manoeuvre for authoritarian systems, especially those like Russia, which sees its security in part in the instability of adversary countries. It's not a new approach: in earlier times it was called subversion.'

Russia has become a regular user of black ops. Russian intelligence, and criminals, can be particularly ruthless. Perhaps it is decades of living under a ruthless police and security machine, beneath which people could not often trust their neighbours or work colleagues, but that machine, enforced by the KGB, appears to have created a particularly brutal culture that even feeds itself into the criminal sphere. Russians have told me that the Russian Mafia is more ruthless than many others. Some told me that, while the Italian Mafia has certain codes of behaviour – one being that they take all reasonable efforts not to kill people in front of their children – the Russian Mafia have no similar compunctions.

Ryan believes that the Russian and Chinese elite see this time in history as a rare opportunity. 'Putin's narratives since the beginning of the war represent a new, invigorated phase of Russian confrontation with Europe and the US. All of his speeches contain some form of narrative about the threat from NATO to Russia. Even if he wanted to wind it back now, I don't think it would be possible for him to do so. But, more broadly … there is, in their view, an inevitable, and at this point irreversible, decline of the West. They see an opportunity now to either hasten this decline, or just to ensure that it occurs. This is playing out across military, information, financial and diplomatic spheres, and is something that western nations have not fully accepted, let alone developed a strategy to arrest. And because western governments have not yet fully accepted this situation, their citizens are being poorly informed about the real threats to their democratic systems and future prosperity and security.'

In general, says Ryan, Western political leaders are unwilling to have tough conversations with their citizens about any topic that leads to disruptive change in either domestic or international affairs. There are no political incentives, or short-term gains, for them to do so. The growing alignment of 'the bad quad authoritarian nations' – Russia, China, Iran and North Korea – is just one such issue.

An increasing closeness between China and Russia has been building over time, but in recent years the two have been much more open about their alliance. In March 2023, as President Xi was leaving Moscow after a visit, he made reference to the dramatically changing world order. He told Putin, 'We are witnessing changes the likeness of which we have not seen for a hundred years, and we are the ones driving these changes together.'

A clearly delighted Putin replied, 'I agree. Have a good trip.'

Xi then said, 'Take care my good friend.' His embrace of Putin was all the more significant given it was more than a year into Russia's war in Ukraine.

As the former Australian ambassador to Moscow, Peter Tesch knows the mindset of Russians and Vladimir Putin well.

Tesch says the war in Ukraine has imposed costs upon Russia that go well beyond any that might have been forecast, both in the numbers of killed and wounded and in the distortive impacts upon the economy and material wellbeing of Russians. He says, 'In vainglorious pursuit of an unrecoverable and illusory imperial past, Putin has mortgaged the future of his country for a generation. The war bears his personal stamp, but the system over which he presides will find it hard to turn from the path he has laid out and the illegal territorial claims he has staked. I doubt, though, that the wider public would prefer prolongation of this costly and pointless tragedy at its expense, but the public's view doesn't determine policy as much in Russia as it might elsewhere. That said, the sudden demise or departure of Putin likely would provide cover for those in Moscow who understand the real, long-term costs to Russia of this insanity, to dial back the conflict, potentially facilitating a ceasefire.'

Western governments, says Tesch, have taken the right decisions to enable Ukraine to fight this war but, he says, they have consistently been too late to have a decisive impact. 'That is at the core of this tragedy. I struggle to understand why the West was so hesitant at the outset. I suspect initially it reflected a view that Russia would prevail swiftly – an assessment as flawed as Russia's of its own prowess. It would be self-delusion as well as potentially a self-fulfilling prophecy to assume that what might come after Putin would be worse, so it is better to strike a deal now. Putin is a rational actor who views the world through a lens different to our own. We fall short in comprehending that world view and devising policies and alternatives that are in our own, and Russia's longer term, interests. Levels of "Russia literacy" are too low, certainly in Australia, to meet this challenge easily.'

Tesch says that Trump's depiction of himself as a maverick and transactional deal maker will unsettle allies and partners and will encourage Putin to seek opportunities to keep advancing Russia's long-term strategic interests as he sees them. As to Russia's real agenda, this can in part can be deduced from Putin's public utterings. Putin's near-term objective, Tesch says, is the reconstitution of the heartland of the old Russian state – what Putin calls *Novorossiya* – which at its core encompasses Belarus and Ukraine. 'More broadly, his avowed goal is "multipolarity", which means replacing the United States at the apex of what Moscow decries as the current "unipolar" global order. Moscow wants to undermine the dominance of the US dollar in global trade and investment. The rhetoric of the October 2024 BRICS summit sets this out in broad terms. Even if it seems unattainable any time soon, it adds complexity and contestability to the established order, which is under growing strain. Russia and China will be key points of this new global compass. What once might have been an opportunistic collaboration now is far more deliberate in its construction and direction, albeit asymmetric in benefit and skewed in China's strategic favour.'

When it comes to Ukraine, few Australians know the country as well as Robert Potter, the former Australian Army officer now assisting Ukrainians to protect their cyber systems. He says if western aid continues to subsidise the fighting strength of the Ukrainian armed forces it's unlikely they will lose. Russian casualties are up dramatically and while Ukraine is losing territory it is doing so very slowly. It is impossible for Russia to continue to expend the resources they are to continue to fight indefinitely. They are starting to run out of armoured vehicles for example. 'I'm probably on the optimistic side,' Potter says, 'but I believe the long-term favours Ukraine. Albeit such a victory would be ruinous for Ukraine and unlikely to be worth the price.'

The key variable is China. 'If they overtly enter the war, either by financially directly subsidising Russia or by sending significant numbers of volunteers, then the war would favour Russian victory.'

But regardless of any ceasefire in Ukraine, Potter believes Russia aims to invade other countries. 'Russia is already intervening in Georgia and Moldova. There have been shipments of FPV [First Person View] drones and military uniforms to Moldova already.' Having said that, Potter does not think that Russia has a longer-term plan, but that both sides – Russia and NATO – 'are just trying to hurt each other as much as possible.'

Australian academic Dr Matthew Sussex has spent considerable time studying Putin. While there has been much discussion about Putin's agenda stopping a NATO expansion, Sussex says in his view Putin's motivation is much more basic: 'Put simply, Putin invaded Ukraine because he wanted to. And his campaigns of meddling and sabotage against the West are about sowing chaos and disunity so that Putin can act with a virtually free hand. As far as Ukraine goes, he likely wants a smaller and battle-scarred Ukraine to become the West's problem, and preferably one that has limited access to the sea.

'He merely shrugged when Finland and Sweden ended decades of neutrality to sign up to NATO membership. Why is Ukraine different?' Sussex thinks it has to do with how synonymous national security is with the security of Putin's regime and with the image Putin has crafted of himself as the guardian of Russian values and culture. On this, Sussex says, 'maybe he has even come to believe [it] himself.'

According to Sussex, Russia considers itself effectively at war with NATO and the broader West. He says, 'I spent some time in Poland in 2024, and some of the stories about Russian disinformation tactics were deeply concerning. Ultimately, I think that Putin will go to any lengths he thinks he can get away with, which includes increasingly violent acts – not only sabotage, but state-sponsored terrorism, often with local goons paid to act as proxies. It's worth noting that we are woefully underprepared for such a campaign here in Australia.'

For many international analysts, Russia's attack on Ukraine reflects the new reality that Russia and its allies, including China, North Korea and Iran, are now prepared to be more aggressive against the US and NATO, which have a waning appetite for maintaining global and regional order. In Sussex's view, 'Trump may change that calculus, but it's just as likely that he changes it for the worse rather than the better. There's also a view that for all his tough talk, Trump is easily swayed by money and is ultimately a coward. I'd expect Russia, China and Iran – plus the DPRK [North Korea] – to test Trump several times.'

Peter Tesch agrees that Russia and its allies are prepared to be more aggressive against the US and NATO. 'Division in western societies and governments – for example over Brexit, immigration, cost of living pressures, and the growth of a national-populist strain in politics – titillates autocrats, who don't face the same constraints of accountability and the need to persuade voters to re-elect them. The Covid pandemic exposed a certain socio-economic fragility and lack of cohesion in some countries, as well as their global supply chain vulnerabilities.'

As to Putin's threats to use nuclear weapons, Sussex says it's unlikely. Russian nuclear doctrine is comparable to that of the US – to use nuclear weapons in order to protect its survival as a nation. 'What's different to the US is that Putin uses nuclear fears as weapons for political warfare. Time and again the Russians have threatened to escalate and hinted at using nukes, so much so that it has become almost like the boy who cried wolf. The trouble is that if it is indeed a bluff, it's virtually impossible to call it. Hence we have to take Russian nuclear threats seriously simply because of the sheer destructive power of the weapons themselves.

'For what it's worth,' he adds, 'I think Putin most likely is bluffing. But he knows the West won't call it, which suits him just fine. At no time in the war has Russia altered its nuclear readiness posture, apart from drills. There's no battlefield utility in using tactical nukes against Ukraine – the broad front means you'd need a lot of them, and Russian troops are ill-equipped to exploit nuclear environments.'

Robert Potter adds to this: 'I think it's pretty clear that Putin understands there would be a kinetic response from NATO [if he escalated to the use of nuclear weapons].'

Peter Tesch believes that the nuclear threat needs to be taken seriously. It is conceivable that Putin could use nuclear weapons in western Ukraine or in a test somewhere in Russia to signal to the world a preparedness to use them. But he says this would provoke global condemnation and seriously erode Moscow's standing, including in countries in the 'Global South' where it seeks greater support. 'Beijing would be profoundly alarmed,' Tesch says, 'not least because it would compel South Korea and Japan to reconsider their own historical disavowal of nuclear weapons. And they wouldn't be alone in this. Triggering nuclear proliferation – potentially also to non-state actors – certainly wouldn't serve Moscow's strategic interests.

'Putin and his mouthpieces have raised the nuclear spectre several dozen times since February 2022, and they, in any case, are not the first to draw the nuclear sabre. Boris Yeltsin growled about this option in 1999, when he took umbrage at US and western criticism of his war in Chechnya. Escalatory talk is part of Moscow's playbook and is hard-wired into a multi-domain approach intended to foster self-deterrence in western governments and societies.'

*

It is vital that the world learns from Russia's invasion of Ukraine. Modern Russia has become a ruthless, brutal machine that no longer observes any traditional international understandings or rules-based order. Yet just as Putin's invasion of Ukraine cemented nationalist Ukrainian sentiment, so too has this new world order contributed to a new appreciation for strategic alliances.

I gained a memorable insight into how Russia is viewed by many in Europe while on a trip to Lithuania in 2023 to cover the NATO conference. While in their capital, Vilnius, it became clear that Putin has become NATO's biggest recruiter.

I met with a 23-year-old Ukrainian who had been provided by the Lithuanian government as a volunteer guide to assist guests of the conference with any questions about the city. This young man sat at a desk in my hotel's reception, eager to help visiting journalists and delegates.

We had several conversations as he told me about the country's history. But what shone through was his support for NATO. He said there was now a surge in support among all Lithuanians – younger ones in particular – for the alliance. Extraordinarily, NATO was now 'cool'. I was surprised to hear such strong support for an alliance that, before Russia's invasion of Ukraine, had been seen as somewhat moribund, if not antiquated.

'If you want to understand the fear of Russia that people in Lithuania and Latvia and Estonia and so many others have, visit the KGB museum here.' He said this with such passion that I did what he urged.

The museum was in an old Stalinist building, and the tour began downstairs in a big basement with all sorts of cells. In particular, one cell had a sunken floor, and at its centre stood an elevated shelf, a metre or so high and just wide enough to sit on. The KGB would fill the sunken area of the cell with water and the prisoner could only sit on the elevated shelf. If the prisoner should ever fall asleep, they would tip into the freezing water, where they would either wake with a start or drown. I found the design that went into this low-cost torture chamber horrifying – it was a diseased creativity that told me everything about the cruel mind of the KGB.

The next morning, I saw the guide again at the hotel reception and told him I'd gone to the museum.

'Now you know why we never want to see Vladimir Putin or any of his other KGB compatriots here in Lithuania,' he said. 'Now you know why for us NATO is everything. I know that in some countries NATO is not considered cool but for us and Latvia and Estonia and smaller European countries NATO is what stands between us and torture.'

At the end of his posting, former American diplomat John Sullivan drew four key points regarding 'the Russian situation' that he says are most relevant to understanding and crafting a strategy to address Putin's war in Ukraine. He warns in very clear terms that a direct military conflict between the US and Russia – the world's two nuclear superpowers – is 'too fraught for humanity, a fact that Putin appears to delight in repeatedly reminding everyone.' Putin and the Kremlin are 'completely untethered from the truth' – as demonstrated by how Putin repeatedly lied when promising Russia would not invade Ukraine. Sullivan's view is that Russia will never truly surrender its aim of subjugating Ukraine and Ukrainians will never give up resisting Russian influence, but that if the US withdraws support for Ukraine it would be 'an historic and epoch-defining mistake'.

Perhaps the most interesting observation Sullivan makes is that the US erred by not engaging Russia and Russians at the end of the Cold War. They were instead distracted by domestic struggles and by various wars in the Middle East, when they should have been doing more to engage and support Russia and the Russian people after the demise of the Soviet Union.

John Sullivan's conclusion is noteworthy. He says the only suitable strategy for the West must be 'a form of 21st century containment' of Russian aggression because Russia will not stop at Ukraine.

*

The future of Ukraine rests largely with Donald Trump. Nobody can be completely sure which course Trump will take – it's possible that he himself does not know. The best guide we have as to what Trump will do is to look at who he is.

Trump is many things, but one thing those who have dealt with him say is that he's transactional – the ultimate deal maker. Angela Merkel, former Chancellor of Germany, says he judges everything 'from the perspective of the property entrepreneur he had been before politics'. Writing in her memoir, *Freedom*, Merkel says, 'Each property could only be allocated once. If he didn't get it, someone else did. That was also how he looked at the world.'

That mindset explains Trump's suggestion that the US should take ownership of Greenland – part of Denmark, a

NATO ally. And his expression that the US should seize control of the Panama Canal and Gaza Strip, and turn Gaza into the 'Riviera of the Middle East'.

When it comes to Ukraine, the other part of Trump's persona that may be a guide is Trump's enthusiasm for 'winners'. It was this widely known view of his proclivities that may well have informed Ukraine's audacious decision to push into Russia and seize Kursk. In a war that Ukraine was slowly losing, 'winning' Kursk from the Russians may well have projected the image that Ukraine was winning when the previous two years suggested otherwise. The taking of Kursk was also driven by the imminent arrival of Trump in that the Ukrainians expected Trump would insist on negotiations and Kursk would give them a stronger hand.

In deciding to play the ultimate deal maker, Trump will need to win over Vladimir Putin. The Ukraine war is, of course, far bigger than Putin. The ruthless KGB mindset that Putin embodies is as entrenched as the man himself. In fact, there are many in the Kremlin who are even more hardline and more hostile to the West than Putin. In this, the disappearance from the stage of Vladmir Vladimirovich Putin will not resolve 'the Russia problem'. Russia is likely to be a de-stabilising and hostile force for at least another generation.

The return of Donald Trump did not augur well for Ukraine. Trump's early phone call to Vladimir Putin was ominous. Firstly, it was a 90-minute call, which appeared to be the beginning of a negotiation – with only one party at the table. The correct procedure would have to set up a call in which the representatives of both countries participated. That way, neither would have felt that they had been disadvantaged. While Volodymyr Zelensky tried to make the best of it, Ukrainian media made clear that he felt he was severely compromised. From then on, Zelensky was a poker player with a bad hand trying to bluff his way to a ceasefire deal.

It would get worse. On 12 February 2025, almost three years to the day since Russia's invasion, Trump's new Secretary of Defence, Peter Hesgeth, gave his first major speech on Ukraine. As he spoke at the Ukraine Defence Contact Group in Brussels, it became clear that he spoke on behalf of the new Trump administration. His comments were so definitive and such a dramatic change from what had operated under the Biden administration.

It was a new world for Ukraine: the bloodshed must stop, the war must stop; European NATO members needed to provide the 'overwhelming' share of lethal and non-lethal aid to Ukraine; there would be no US troops deployed to Ukraine; it was 'an illusory goal' to think that Ukraine could return to the borders it had before 2014 and this would only prolong the war, which meant Ukraine would not be getting Crimea back from Russia. And finally, the cruelest cut of all – 'the United

States does not believe that NATO membership for Ukraine is a realistic outcome of a negotiated settlement.'

With those comments, the new Trump administration devastated Ukrainians. The US was clearly stepping away from the war, and the Europeans were being told that it was largely over to them to try to keep the Russians at bay. But Ukrainians also knew that the three years of their nationwide citizen's defence had not been wasted. They'd stopped Vladimir Putin taking their capital, and were at least able to walk into negotiations still in control of much of their country. They had not collapsed in the face of Russian aggression.

However, Ukrainians also know that even once a ceasefire has been negotiated this will not be the end of their war with Russia. They know Russia better than anyone. They know the true nature of the heart of the leadership of modern Russia – not just of Putin and his KGB compatriots but the entire hierarchy of the Kremlin.

The ending of this war does not solve Ukraine's problem. It's now clearer than ever to Ukrainians that they have a neighbour who they can never be completely comfortable with.

This book documents some of the extraordinary efforts of ordinary Ukrainians to save their country. It's clear that many powerful people in neighbouring Russia do not believe that Ukraine should be a sovereign country. It's clear that many powerful people in the Kremlin want to drag Ukraine into a new Russian Empire. But in Vladimir Putin's brutal attempt to take Ukraine by force, Putin has done the very opposite of what he intended to do. Due to the extraordinary efforts of millions of Ukrainians – from aging punk rockers and former brand managers, to university lecturers and engineering students – the Ukrainian identity has seen a huge resurgence.

Inside Ukraine, the Ukrainian language has taken over where once Russian was widely spoken. Ukrainian culture has risen to a new prominence. Ukrainian singers are proudly competing on the world stage. The Ukrainian flag is now held with a pride not seen for decades. While still in the midst of one of the bloodiest wars in modern times, Ukraine is still standing. The future will not be easy, and nothing is guaranteed. But Ukraine strides forward more determined and more united than ever.

Ukrainians know the Russian language as well as they know Ukrainian – in some cases better. They know from the way Russians have changed their language during the course of this war that they were in for a long, bitter and perhaps inter-generational battle.

When a country is at war, the language that its media and leaders use reveals underlying realities. After Hamas broke into Israel on 7 October 2023 and committed its atrocities, I flew to Israel to interview leading figures in Israel's defence establishment. One of them was Ehud Barak, a former Prime Minister and one of the country's most decorated soldiers.

Mid-way through an interview in 2024 about Israel's war in Gaza following Hamas's 7 October attacks, Barak told me something intriguing: 'There is no word in Hebrew for accountability.' It was Barak's way of trying to explain how the concept of accountability in Israel was different from the concept in many other countries.

After Russia's full-scale invasion, President Zelensky's language changed. He made hundreds of addresses to his people, but in all those speeches he rarely used the word 'I'. This was a marked difference from the candidate and president Zelensky who had used 'I' as much as any politician. After his country came under attack by the Russians, Zelensky effectively extinguished the word 'I' from his lexicon – the personal pronoun giving way to 'we'.

The language in Russia also changed. Former Australian intelligence analyst Kyle Wilson was a senior officer in the Office of National Assessments for many years. His proficiency in Russian is of such a level that, three times, he has been asked by the Australian government to translate conversations between Putin and Australian politicians – including twice when Prime Minister Tony Abbott had phone conversations with Putin in the wake of the shooting down of the Malaysian plane MH17 in 2014, in which 38 Australians died.

Wilson still monitors Russia's media. He points to a famous Russian saying, 'In war, as in war.' As he observes: 'In other words, "In war everything goes." And there is clear evidence that Russia has been torturing people in this war in Ukraine.'

In recent years Wilson has noticed something that few others would have picked up – the disappearance from the Russian language of the word *miloserdie*, which is drawn from two other words, *milo* (nice) and *serdie* (heart). Literally 'a nice heart', but it takes the more common meaning we find in our use of the word 'mercy'.

The wider question is this: What should the world do when one of the most powerful countries in the world – a country with more nuclear warheads than any other country – no longer has a word for mercy?

ACKNOWLEDGEMENTS

There are many people to thank for their contribution to *A Bunker in Kyiv*. The first are all the extraordinary Ukrainians who told me and Sylvie their stories. The word hero is too often used in the media to the point where it has sometimes become a cliché, but these people fit that definition – they have rallied to defend their country against one of the most powerful and ruthless armies in the world. They have adapted their lives to join a war effort against Vladimir Putin. Almost every person we met had asked themselves: what can we do to help Ukraine?

Their stories are inspirational. Musicians who have become world-class drone makers. A 27-year-old university lecturer who's galvanised his students to turn up to an old warehouse each night and turn agricultural drones into kamikaze drones. A 23-year-old who travels across de-occupied areas handing out cameras to children so that they can document their war and then be able to talk about it. A company marketing manager who watched from his apartment on 22 February 2022 as Russian missiles hit Kyiv and, along with his brother, turned up to the army recruitment office that day to enlist, suddenly finding himself the commander of a unit. An academic who re-arranged the schedules of her lecturers so see could continue to lecture using an iPad in a trench on the frontline. And there are many non-Ukrainians who have joined the effort – including a 23-year-old from Maitland, Australia, who ran a whipper-snipper and gutter-cleaning business, who saw Ukrainian president Volodymyr Zelensky on television and told his mother he was off to the front line. He'd never been overseas and did not own a passport. A few months later he was sitting in a foxhole in the middle of a Ukrainian winter trying to spot Russian soldiers through the darkness.

Enormous thanks also to the brilliant team at HarperCollins/ABC Books. A special thanks to Helen Littleton. Just as she believed in our previous book, *Balcony Over Jerusalem*, Helen was immediately moved by our proposal to tell the stories of ordinary Ukrainians fighting the might of the Russian army. Helen's love of books, stories and storytellers is clear the moment you meet her. Helen backs her authors and their stories. Her outstanding team has been equally supportive: senior editor Shannon Kelly ensured that the commissioning and editing process was not just painless but enjoyable; Simone Ford gave magnificent care and forensic attention to the manuscript; and Hannah Lynch, as always, works tirelessly to ensure the team's books and authors have opportunities to take their books to as wide an audience as possible. Deep gratitude also to Georgia Frances King, who took early carriage of the project and then, towards the end, assisted by casting her smart journalistic eye over the first draft and making some brilliant suggestions. Thanks also to Gaby Naher, my literary agent who so expertly set up meetings with key publishers to allow us to explain the project. Her connections and love of books and writing opens many doors. I also owe thanks to David Robinson and Robert Potter, two former Australian army officers who allowed me to join them in Kyiv as they met the highest levels of Ukraine's military, intelligence and political figures as part of their efforts to help them to fend off Russia's cyber attacks.

And finally, to my co-author Sylvie Le Clezio. This was, for us, another huge adventure. *Balcony Over Jerusalem* was a life-changing adventure as we spent six years in the Middle East trying to learn what truly motivated all the various countries and groupings. And this new book is another great adventure. As we boarded an overnight train in Poland for Kyiv, the challenge of telling the stories of a people under the pressure of war loomed large. Sylvie, a documentary filmmaker, had a huge number of ideas and was keen and thoughtful about how we should tell the remarkable stories of Ukrainians writing themselves into history as they fended off Putin's army. Sylvie's ability to win the trust of so many Ukrainians from different backgrounds, as well as her formidable research and investigation, has underpinned much of this book.

And finally, to you, the reader, for your interest. One of the worst things that can happen to Ukrainians is that the world grows weary of their existential battle. Such fatigue would play into Putin's hands. By continuing to read about and discuss Putin's atrocities, we all help to inoculate the world as much as possible against Putin's real agenda: to march across Europe to reclaim the Russian empire.

ENDNOTES

1   John Lyons 'Hackers Inc: Chasing the cybercrime syndicates attacking Australia', *Four Corners*, 17 April 2023, https://www.abc.net.au/news/2023-04-17/hackers-inc:-chasing-the-cybercrime-syndicates/102233374

2   John Lyons, *Balcony Over Jerusalem: A Middle East Memoir*, HarperCollins, 2017 and re-released 2024.

3   Winston Churchill, 2 June 1940, https://winstonchurchill.org/resources/speeches/1940-the-finest-hour/we-shall-fight-on-the-beaches/

4   White House Press Briefing, Press Secretary Jen Psaki and National Security Advisor Jake Sullivan, 11 February 2022.

5   *Reuters*, 'Timeline: The events leading up to the Russia's invasion of Ukraine', 28 February 2022, https://www.reuters.com/world/europe/events-leading-up-russias-invasion-ukraine-2022-02-28/

6   Janelle Miles, 'Daryna Povorozniuk fled Ukraine when she was heavily pregnant, but has found safety and support in Brisbane', *ABC News*, 18 June 2023, https://www.abc.net.au/news/2023-06-18/ukrainian-refugees-get-help-in-brisbane-mater-hospital/102487372

7   *BBC TV*, 'Russia's borders does not end anywhere', https://www.bbc.com/news/world-europe-38093468

8   *Meduza*, 'Russia's sprawling wartime fake news machine', https://meduza.io/en/feature/2023/09/25/russia-s-sprawling-wartime-fake-news-machine

9   *Reuters*, 'Top brands pull out of Russia but their goods remain easy to find', https://meduza.io/en/feature/2023/09/25/russia-s-sprawling-wartime-fake-news-machine

10 *Carnegie Politika*, 'How the latest sanctions will impact Russia – and the world', June 2024.

11 Sam Everingham and Kerry Duncan, *Surrogacy Stories: Twenty Extraordinary Journeys to Parenthood*, Stethoscope Research, 2022.

12 *The Cancer Letter*, 'Three weeks in Mariupol; How Dr Hanych kept his cancer patients alive amid Russia's attack', August 2022, https://cancerletter.com/the-cancer-letter/20220805_1/

13 Daryna Hrysiuk, 'Behind Blue Eyes project: children's dreams and creativity against the backdrop of war', 29 April 2024, https://war.ukraine.ua/articles/behind-blue-eyes-project-children-s-dreams-and-creativity-against-the-backdrop-of-war/

14 Lyons, 'Hackers Inc', op cit.

15 https://www.youtube.com/watch?v=P8OBR9yigFA (video no longer available).

16 Gallagher Fenwick, *Volodymyr Zelensky: Ukraine in the Blood*, LITOS, 2022, page 13.

17 Ariane Chemin, 'For Volodymyr Zelensky, politics was a fiction that begame his reality', *Le Monde*, 21 February 2023 https://www.lemonde.fr/en/international/article/2023/02/21/for-volodymyr-zelensky-politics-was-a-fiction-that-became-his-reality_6016731_4.html

18 Fenwick, op cit, page 10.

19 Jamie Dettmer, 'The strengths and weaknesses of Volodymyr Zelenskyy', Politico, 27 February 2023, https://www.politico.eu/article/strength-weaknesse-ukraine-president-volodymyr-zelenskyy/

20 Poutine et les présidents français réalisé par Bertrand Coq et Élodie Duboscq. LCI, La Chaine Info, https://www.youtube.com/watch?v=DgTkt4pUBcs.

21 Ibid.

22 Michel Eltchaninoff, *Inside the mind of Vladimir Putin*, Hurst, 2017.

23 'Putin's Own Vodka Brand Netted Him $500 Million – Investigation', The Moscow Times, 28 February 2023, https://www.themoscowtimes.com/2023/02/28/putins-own-vodka-brand-netted-him-500-million-investigation-a80360

24 Vera Grantseva, *Les Russes veulent-ils la Guerre?*, 2023

25 *The Bell*, 'How the Kremlin's internet propaganda HQ operates', 2023, https://en.thebell.io/how-the-kremlins-internet-propaganda-hq-operates/

26 Letter read by Ukrainian ambassador Sergiy Kyslytsya to United Nations, UNTV, 1 March 2022.

27 Gary Kasparov, @kasparov63, X (formerly Twitter), 24 June 2023.

28 Anastasiia Carrier, 'Revealed: Vladimir Putin's secret Black Sea bunker', *Business Insider*, 17 May 2023,. https://www.businessinsider.com/revealed-vladimir-putins-secret-black-sea-bunker-russia-kremlin-palace-2023-5

29 *Frontline*, 'Putin and the Presidents', Season 2023, Episode 10, PBS, 31 January 2023, https://www.pbs.org/wgbh/frontline/documentary/putin-and-the-presidents/